The Meditations of
Marcus Aurelius

Other Books in the SkyLight Illuminations Series

The Meditations of Marcus Aurelius

Selections Annotated & Explained

Annotation by
Russell McNeil, PhD

Translation by
George Long;
Revised by
Russell McNeil, PhD

Walking Together, Finding the Way ®
SKYLIGHT PATHS®
PUBLISHING
Woodstock, Vermont

The Meditations of Marcus Aurelius:
Selections Annotated & Explained

2012 Quality Paperback Edition, Fourth Printing

Library of Congress Cataloging-in-Publication Data
Marcus Aurelius, Emperor of Rome, 121–180.
[Meditations. English. Selections]
The meditations of Marcus Aurelius : selections annotated & explained / annotation by Russell McNeil ; translation by George Long ; revised by Russell McNeil.
 p. cm. — (SkyLight illuminations)
Includes bibliographical references.
ISBN-13: 978-1-59473-236-2 (quality pbk.)
ISBN-10: 1-59473-236-1 (quality pbk.)
1. Ethics. 2. Stoics. 3. Life. I. McNeil, Russell. II. Long, George, 1800–1879. III. Title.
B581.M36 2007
188—dc22
                                                        2007028506

10 9 8 7 6 5 4
Manufactured in the United States of America
Cover design: Walter C. Bumford III, Stockton, Massachusetts
Cover art: Equestrian statue of Marcus Aurelius

SkyLight Paths Publishing is creating a place where people of different spiritual traditions come together for challenge and inspiration, a place where we can help each other understand the mystery that lies at the heart of our existence.

SkyLight Paths sees both believers and seekers as a community that increasingly transcends traditional boundaries of religion and denomination—people wanting to learn from each other, *walking together, finding the way.*

SkyLight Paths, "Walking Together, Finding the Way," and colophon are trademarks of LongHill Partners, Inc., registered in the U.S. Patent and Trademark Office.

Walking Together, Finding the Way®
Published by SkyLight Paths Publishing
A Division of LongHill Partners, Inc.
Sunset Farm Offices, Route 4, P.O. Box 237
Woodstock, VT 05091
Tel: (802) 457-4000   Fax: (802) 457-4004
www.skylightpaths.com

Contents □

4 Stoicism and the Body

5 Stoicism and the Mind

6 The Method of Stoicism

7 Stoicism and the Environment

8 The Practice of Stoicism

Acknowledgments ☐

To my grandmother Mamie Addicott, who taught me to laugh and to love music. To my grandfather William Russell McNeil, who labored with dignity for fifty years underground in the coal mines of Cape Breton, and who taught me to love geometry. To my colleagues and friends at Vancouver Island University; the University of Nevada, Las Vegas; and the University of Victoria: Ian Johnston for inspiration; John Black for trust and friendship; Maureen Okun for poetry and precision; Norm Cameron for skepticism and eclecticism; Janina Hornosty for insight and integrity; Lisa MacLean for creativity; Maggie McColl for valuing science; Gwyneth Evans for sensitivity; Libby McGrattan for taking care of us all; Kayley Vernalis (now at Cal State U, LA) for philosophy and art; Len Zane (UNLV) for physics; Bill Weller for astronomy; and David S. Scott (U Vic) for vision. To my children, Liam, Bronwyn, and Rose Siubhan, who taught me to love life. To Madeleine Ware, who supported me throughout all of this. To Mark Ogilbee, my SkyLight Paths editor, who believed I could do this. And to Marcus Aurelius, who labored to make us all free so long ago. Here are his words:

> Always observe how ephemeral and worthless human things are, and what was yesterday a little mucous tomorrow will be a mummy or ashes. Pass then through this little space of time conformably to nature, and end your journey in contentment, just as an olive falls off when it is ripe, blessing nature who produced it, and thanking the tree on which it grew.
>
> —IV:48

Introduction □

The *Meditations* of Roman emperor Marcus Aurelius Antoninus (121–180 CE) is not a religious work or a sacred text or even a philosophical treatise on Stoicism. The original material consisted of roughly four hundred relatively short personal notes written over ten years and scattered in twelve journals composed in no particular order—much of it repetitive. In spite of this, the *Meditations* is widely read today by people from all walks of life and used by many in the regulation of their personal lives, in businesses, and even in the conduct of government. For many people, the *Meditations* is life changing. The intensely personal quality of the writing mirrors the soul of a deeply compassionate man who expressed his ideas with penetrating tenderness, intelligence, and honesty.

This book will show you how to reason like a Stoic. Although Stoicism is no longer considered a living philosophy, it has as much significance today as it did two thousand years ago. The strength of Stoicism resides in its reverence for that unique human capacity called *reason*. Most of the personal, political, and environmental troubles we face at the dawn of this century come not from the exercise of human reason but from its abuse—in the guise of power and passion. Stoicism offers psychological and spiritual remedies in all three areas by showing us how we can address our contemporary troubles.

Stoicism is not a religion. It is an ancient philosophical system with profound spiritual consequences. The word *stoic,* when used today, has come to refer to those people who *appear* indifferent to or unaffected by the emotional experiences of pleasure or pain. This indeed was a characteristic in those who held Stoicism as a philosophy. But this mental attitude is also characteristic of Buddhism, which like Stoicism, also advocates the restriction of desires and the control of suffering. For a true Stoic (and a true Buddhist), these mental attitudes are *genuine* and a means to their respective philosophical goals. For a Buddhist, the eventual goal is enlightenment. For the Stoic the goal is a different sort of enlightenment, better expressed as happiness or joy *in this life*. Although the popular image of Stoicism is one of stiff indifference, the Stoicism of the ancient world was a surprisingly friendly and compassionate system with remarkable relevance in our times.

"The Most Beautiful Figure in History"

Marcus Aurelius was one of history's great spokespersons for Stoicism, and he captured the tenets of the philosophy in his personal journals. In his review of an 1862 English-language translation of the *Meditations* by George Long (1800–1879), the renowned English poet and literary critic Matthew Arnold (1822–1888)[1] described the world's first and only "philosopher king" as "the most beautiful figure in history." A century earlier in his *The Decline and Fall of the Roman Empire*, the famed historian Edward Gibbon (1737–1794) characterized the reign of Aurelius as the "only period in history when the *happiness* of a great people was the sole object of government." This great and gentle man died in Vindobona (now Vienna) in 180 CE—from either the plague or, possibly, according to an account by Roman historian Cassius Dio (c. 155–c. 229), from poisons administered on the orders of his allegedly illegitimate son, the tyrant coemperor Commodus (161–192). With Aurelius's death, the formal four-hundred-year history of Stoic philosophy, a movement that had reached its culmination in his *Meditations*, ended. The premature decline of Stoicism coincided with the beginning of the fall of Rome. Within three hundred years, the empire would be no more. But the ideas of Stoicism lived on, as fodder for a hundred newer philosophies, and in their appropriated forms as explanatory interpretations for the rising sect called Christianity then sweeping the Western world. You will see many parallels and intriguing similarities between

Christianity and Stoicism in this book. Christianity is a religion, but its focus, like Stoicism, is on love. Stoicism and Christianity both promise happiness in return for a life of virtue. But the reward for Christian virtue is reserved for life in another Kingdom, in a life after death. Stoicism, in contrast, was a philosophy with temporal spiritual consequences. There is no life after death for the Stoic. The reward for Stoic virtue is now, and in this life.

The Five Good Emperors

Marcus Aurelius was the last of the "Five Good Emperors," five extraordinary men who had governed the Roman world at the apex of that great empire's imperial power and influence. Their names (and the years they ruled) were Nerva (96–98), Trajan (98–117), Hadrian (117–138), Antoninus Pius (138–161), and Marcus Aurelius (161–180). For more than two centuries, during a historical period called the *Pax Romana* (Roman Peace), beginning with the reign of Augustus Caesar (27 BCE–14 CE) and right up to the death of Aurelius, the Roman world had enjoyed unprecedented prosperity and peace. The civil wars that had ravaged the early empire were three centuries in her past. The perpetual bloodshed and invasions that began after the end of the *Pax Romana* were to end with the final collapse of the empire in the West within three centuries.

Edward Gibbon described the last forty-two years of the *Pax Romana*, the years coincident with the reigns of the two Antonines (Antoninus Pius and Marcus Aurelius Antoninus), as a period governed by the rule of genuine "wisdom and virtue," values exhibited in abundance by both of these noble men.

Marcus Aurelius was three years old when his father, Marcus Annius Verus, a Praetor (a head of the judiciary) died in 124 CE. After his father died, Aurelius was raised by his paternal grandfather, also named Marcus Annius Verus (48–138), who died in 138 at the age of ninety. His grandfather had held the ranks of consul (three times) and prefect of Rome. There were normally two consuls who served as joint heads of state and commanders in chief of the army. A prefect was an appointed position, and there were many of these.

After the death of his grandfather, Aurelius, who was then sixteen, was adopted by the future emperor Antoninus Pius. That adoption was requested by then-emperor Hadrian (76–138), who wanted one day to see Aurelius as emperor, and who made the adoption a condition of Antoninus's future accession. Antoninus Pius admired and loved the young Aurelius, as had Hadrian before him, and Pius later proudly gave his daughter Faustina (c.127–175) in marriage to Aurelius. After Aurelius succeeded Pius in 161, and at his own insistence, he shared the first eight years of his reign with his adoptive brother Lucius Verus (130–169), the eldest natural son of Pius. As coemperor, Lucius Verus willingly assumed a secondary role. Lucius Verus died in 169. Aurelius then ruled as sole emperor for nine years, until 177, before elevating his son Commodus to the rank of coemperor. Aurelius died three years later, in his fifty-ninth year.

The Character of Marcus Aurelius

From all accounts, Marcus Aurelius dedicated his rule exclusively to the service of his subjects. Edward Gibbon captured the character of Aurelius with these words: "He was severe to himself, indulgent to the imperfection of others, just and beneficent to all mankind." Gibbon acknowledges also that Aurelius detested war, as a "disgrace and calamity of human nature." But when war was necessary in the defense of the empire from invading Germanic tribes, "[Aurelius] readily exposed his person to eight winter campaigns on the frozen banks of the Danube." Aurelius was the only true philosopher king in human history. His rule was the only time in history when ethical theory and practice converged without compromise within a practical worldly administration. What Aurelius came to believe in his Stoic philosophy, he mirrored in his administration. He was a true champion of the poor, and he opposed slavery. He also founded philosophical schools, orphanages, and hospitals, and when revenues were needed for war he refused to raise taxes, preferring instead to auction off his own personal possessions. He tolerated the Roman gladiatorial traditions, but ordered combatants to use only blunted weapons.

Faustina and Commodus

As fine and gentle and courageous and intelligent as Aurelius was, he was indeed indulgent, a character trait that Gibbon attributed to "the unsuspecting goodness of his heart." The man that Protestant theologian Reinhold Niebuhr (1892–1971) once called "the noblest character of his time," was, it seems at times, also easily deceived by the two people closest to him in life, his beloved wife and his sole surviving son, Commodus. His wife Faustina had been Aurelius's first and only love. While Aurelius reputedly was loyal to Faustina during the thirty years of their marriage, she had been notorious in antiquity for her many infidelities, although the veracity of some of those ancient accounts is disputed by some. In his *Meditations,* Aurelius in fact praised Faustina for her affectionate nature, her obedience, and her down-to-earth simplicity. In carrying out her official duties as empress, Faustina remained always by her husband's side, courageously accompanying him on many of his military campaigns. She was killed in an accident while on one of those expeditions in 175. Aurelius grieved her death and celebrated her life by opening several charity orphanages for girls in her name and renaming the city where she died after her.

Gibbon is less generous in his assessment of Faustina: "Marcus was the only man in the empire who seemed ignorant or insensible of the irregularities of Faustina." Those "irregularities" had cast doubt on the legitimacy of at least one of the thirteen children (including two sets of twins) of their marriage—their only surviving son and heir Commodus, whose real father was rumored to be one of Faustina's gladiator lovers.

Commodus ruled jointly with Aurelius from 177 to 180. Although Aurelius spared nothing in his many attempts to expand the mind of the young Commodus by doing everything in his power to prepare him for his imperial duties, those attempts were fruitless. Commodus was to become his saddest legacy. Commodus's excesses as emperor surpassed those of some of the worst tyrants of history, including those of the incestuous despot emperor Caligula (12–41). Commodus seemed to have had no redeeming qualities other than his famous gladiatorial skills, but even in those his brutality was legendary. The biographer of Commodus was blunt in his assessment. "[Commodus was] base, shameless, cruel, lecherous, defiled, and debauched." Commodus's tyranny lasted for a dreadful thirteen years before an athletic domestic (a youthful wrestler named Narcissus) strangled him in his bath after he had been poisoned at the hand of his favorite concubine, Marcia, who feared that she too might soon become one of the emperor's many bloody victims.

The *Meditations*

Aurelius wrote his *Meditations* in Greek while on military campaigns against invading Germanic tribes between 170–180 CE. Although Aurelius organized the original material into twelve books, he never collated the passages in any thematic way. It appears that the material was used as he intended, as a method for personal self-study and reflection. There is no evidence of any attempt on his part to publish these. Aurelius regarded himself more as a teacher than as an original philosopher. But he did often lecture on Stoicism as emperor, and he took it to be his moral duty to live his life according to the Stoic ideals he espoused in his journals. The only complete copy of the original manuscript is in the Vatican Library. The first copy of the work did not appear in book form until 1558. The first English translation was published in London in 1692 under the imposing title, *The meditations of Marcus Aurelius Antoninus the Roman emperor, concerning himself. Treating of a natural man's happiness: wherein it consisteth, and of the means to attain unto it.* As cumbersome as that title is, it does capture the essence of the *Meditations.* It is a work about the seemingly illusive human quest for happiness, what happiness truly is, and what we as human beings must do to be happy. The answers are surprising, as we will see below. Because it was written as a personal journal, there is no systematic or thematic presentation in the *Meditations*, and many of the passages repeat ideas developed elsewhere. For this volume, I have chosen to order selections by theme, with the first five parts focusing on the Stoic concepts of happiness, virtue, vice, the body, and the mind. These are designed as a preparation for a clearer understanding of the method of Stoicism described in part 6. The last three parts are devoted to ways in which Stoic practice and thinking apply in our attitude toward the environment (part 7), in practical personal life (part 8), and in the wider social, political, and business community (part 9).

The Stoic Answer

In his *Meditations*, Marcus Aurelius notes that human life is insignificant and short. But for Aurelius, human life can also be rich and joyful for those who follow clear moral guidelines. These rules also come from an authority. This authority is internal, but strangely, it is shared with every human being on the planet. We can also learn these rules on our own through meditation—that is, earnest reflection and contemplation. In doing so, we can feel secure in the certain knowledge that the actions we take in adhering to these rules and principles are right and just and good for everyone. In following this path, Aurelius is confident that we will secure happiness and freedom, and do so in this life, and that this happiness will endure throughout all of this life no matter what fate or misfortune befalls us.

You may wonder how Aurelius developed this stunning perspective. In his writings, he tells us quite clearly, and he even shows us how we, too, can come to the same conclusions. There is enough material in this book for you to experiment, if only tentatively, with the process Aurelius used. There is no attempt here to "convert" you to Stoicism. Stoicism is a philosophical orientation, not a religion, but it is an orientation with spiritual consequences. If you find yourself in agreement with each step in the Stoic process, you might find yourself forever trapped in a state of sublime tranquility—but that's the only risk you face.

The Perspective of a Physicist

My academic training was in physics, and it was this background that first attracted me to Stoicism, a philosophy that was grounded firmly on the nature of the physical world as understood in ancient times. I studied theoretical particle physics in graduate school and later helped pioneer a laser radar (LIDAR) technology that has since been successfully deployed on the surface of Mars (NASA Phoenix mission). In a later period of my career, I worked on technologies involving the use of hydrogen as a renewable energy source. But for most of the past two decades, I was a university college professor in a multidisciplinary liberal studies department, where I worked with teams of fellow academics from English, philosophy, art history, political science, economics, and other fields. Although we came from different backgrounds, we all did the same thing. We lectured on the same books and led seminars on the same topics. The books we all read focused mainly on differing aspects of the problem I've posed for you in this introduction: How should we live our lives? One of those books was *Meditations* by Marcus Aurelius. The others included works from Homer to Mark Twain, from Machiavelli to Simone de Beauvoir. My role as a teacher was not to direct my students to right answers but rather to encourage them to read these books, think about them, and use their reason to make up their own minds. I am not going to change my advice now for you, but I will tell you that Aurelius was always a favorite, for me and for my students. Students said and wrote many things about Aurelius, but the one thing they said most about him was that they *loved* what he had to say, and that they *loved* him. I agreed. I still do.

The Role of Attitude and Opinion

The seventeenth-century English philosopher Thomas Hobbes (1588–1679) characterized human life as solitary, poor, nasty, brutish, and short. Life may be short, but for Aurelius life was not necessarily solitary, poor, nasty, or brutish. Those qualities for Aurelius are not a matter of fact, but a matter of our attitude toward our circumstances, and attitude is a matter of choice. We have the power to change our opinion about anything—including the opinions that our lives are solitary or poor or nasty or brutish. This shifting of opinions is not based on denial, as some might suspect. It comes instead from a shift in values. We feel poor, for example, because we have no money. We feel life is nasty and solitary when we lose our health or our loved ones to tragedy. But these feelings of poverty, loneliness, and grief rest on the beliefs (opinions) that money and health and our relationships are the values that give life its meaning. What would it be like for us if we were to discover that the values that give meaning to life were not these things? What would it be like for us if the things that give meaning were things we knew we could not lose and if somehow we came to know this with certainty?

For Aurelius it is the insignificance of our infinitely brief present life, embedded as it is between the two infinities of past and future, that gives real meaning to our lives. That meaning is as sweet and gentle and comforting and courageous as the voice of the man who speaks to us in his *Meditations.* And this voice speaks from a time not unlike our time, as the first major cracks that led to the eventual fall of the Roman Empire began to appear; it speaks with a voice formed within a social confusion and fear of terror not unlike the social confusion and fear of terror of our age that began with the tragic events of September 11, 2001. The voice that offered comfort and meaning in the troubled Roman world might well offer equivalent comfort and meaning in our lives today. The Stoicism of Aurelius has not lost its meaning or relevance. It was, and I believe still can be, a living philosophy with meaningful spiritual implications. But it is rooted in a deeply rational argument—an argument that is not contingent upon religious faith, or authority, or divine revelation—but instead is founded on a method that invites each of us to discover and to explore nature, and to do this on our own terms. In doing this, as Aurelius explained, the rules of engagement we so desperately crave in our modern world now will reveal themselves to us. In following those rules we can discover the happiness and freedom we all desire and deserve.

The Ruling Principle of Nature

For Aurelius, our only duty is to live in conformity with what he calls our "ruling principle"—the native intelligence that lies at the heart of our human capacity to reason. This duty is common to all people, because it comes from a universal and shared intelligence that is the heart of the natural world. This natural world, as Aurelius understood it, is comprised of two material principles. One of these he calls the active principle, the other, the passive. These two principles are the basis of an ancient Stoic physics that divide the materials of nature into two different types: ordinary matter and a finer material the Stoics call *pneuma* (breath). Ordinary matter is passive because matter itself is essentially static. Intermixed with matter is *pneuma*, which is the agent of animation and is therefore active. Everything in nature is a mixture of these two physical materials.

In human beings, the Stoics associate *pneuma* with the soul or mind, and associate its actions with reason or the ruling principle of the mind. On a larger scale, the sum total of all the *pneuma* of the universe (from which the human soul is derived) is associated with a universal or divine intelligence called *Logos* (word), and the Stoic concept of God. A parallel passive-active dichotomy survives in the modern age in the division of the world into matter (atoms and molecules—a passive principle) and the laws that govern the complex interactions of matter (the forces and fields of physics—an active principle). According to Aurelius, the active ruling principle of the universe (also called divine reason) directs nature—like a god—but unlike the God of the Judeo-Christian tradition, this principle is not above nature, creating and controlling it, but embedded in and part of nature.

What Is Good?

The ruling principle that directs our human nature comes to us directly from the ruling intelligence of nature. It is, in fact, the same stuff but only part of the whole. This is the principle that is responsible for our human capacity for reason and logic because it comes from the universal source of all reason, which is divine. For Aurelius, the ruling intelligence in nature is the standard for what he calls good. This may seem a strange use for the word *good,* but his argument is compelling. When we look at nature and observe its laws, we will see that those laws appear to be flawless. Those laws—even if we do not fully understand their details—seem to work perfectly. In no sense is it meaningful or sensible to say that the laws of nature could somehow be better than they are. If the laws cannot be improved, they must be perfect. That is what my reasoning tells me.

Aurelius goes a step further and equates the perfection of nature's laws with beauty. When human beings call something beautiful, they do so because it meets some standard for perfection, at least in their own minds. But for Aurelius the ultimate standard for beauty is not something subjective. For Aurelius, if something is truly beautiful, it will be truly beautiful to everyone, and this is what makes it truly good. In regular human experience people have different standards for beauty. My standards and yours may differ—and as a consequence, so too may the things we believe are good for us. But from Aurelius's perspective, the laws of nature represent a gold standard for beauty and goodness both. For Aurelius this is a standard that all people would be compelled to accept—if only they would look. This argument rests at the heart of Aurelius's *Meditations* and the method of Stoicism. In revealing herself to us, nature, rightly understood, demonstrates for us what it means to be good.

Living According to Nature

Because the ruling intelligence is synonymous with the laws of nature and is therefore good, we too are good when we act in accord with this same ruling intelligence—or in other words, in accord with nature. It follows that *we ought to live according to nature.* Living in accord with nature requires far more from us than obeying the law of gravity. The three principles Aurelius extracts from his observations of nature go further than the laws of physics. First, human beings are essentially social.

Second, the passive aspect of human life, the physical body, is secondary to its active aspect, the mind and its power of reason. Third, the mind is governed by perfect law and is therefore immune from external harm. These ideas need further expansion, but this is one of the first assertions in the West of environmental interconnectedness and interdependence that ties all-to-one and one-to-all through a benign universal intelligence or divine reason.

In a figurative way, this cosmos-as-nature principle, as voiced through Aurelius, reflects nature as a single ecosystem. Nature is in this sense perfect because the laws of nature (which even we moderns may still be only dimly aware of) are good. Of course, it is possible for anyone who studies nature to agree that the laws of nature are amazing (perhaps even perfect, in a manner of speaking) and that they may be somehow good, but tying these ideas to human morality might seem a bit of a stretch. Yet this is what Aurelius does. And he does it in a way that compels us to examine the possibility that our moral nature is linked to the nature that produced us, and that nature can teach us the rules of engagement with life. Perhaps there are flaws in the arguments Aurelius provides. But they are arguments and they are based on reason—and reason is something we all possess—and these arguments are challenging to refute. Reading the *Meditations* does not demand a conversion, or special faith, or an acceptance of the wisdom of a long dead prophet. Aurelius was a philosopher, not a prophet. He is dead, but his ideas are very much alive. His ideas offer a remarkable degree of consistency and straightforward commonsense logic. The philosophy is very accessible; he meant it to be so. Academic training is not a prerequisite.

The Divinity of Nature

As insignificant as we humans are when measured against space and time, it is hard to deny that we are inescapably in nature; we also come from nature; and we will inevitably return to nature. From the perspective of Marcus Aurelius, the sacredness of life is defined in our integrated connection with the universal intelligence, the active principle of nature. From cradle to grave, the universality of laws that govern nature, of which we are a part, manifest their perfection in us. We are subject to the same mechanical, gravitational, and electrochemical forces that govern the movements of the stars. Aurelius always associates the governing principle of nature as mild and embracing and identifies this power as female and mother:

> To her who gives and takes back all, to nature, the man or woman who is instructed and modest says, Give what you will; take back what you will. And these words are said not proudly, but obediently and from a pleasure with her.
>
> —X:14

Aurelius maintains that personal tranquility comes to us when we act in conformity with nature through a virtuous act, such as reaching out with compassion to someone in distress. The benefits extend beyond personal satisfaction. Living with nature has collateral implications. Because every human being is connected through his or her common genesis in the divine principle of nature, what is good for one is good for all. Freedom and happiness rest solely in actions performed in conformity with nature, because those actions conform to the divine and eternal in us. A life according to nature is a life free of self-interest because it conforms to our duty to be social, one of the three fundamental principles of Stoic practice discussed above.

A Brief History of Stoicism

Stoicism as a distinct philosophical school began near the end of the fourth century BCE in Athens under Zeno of Citium (333–264 BCE). The movement takes its name from the Stoa, a painted corridor on one side of the marketplace in Athens where the early members would meet. The subsequent history of this movement is usually divided into three periods: the old Stoa dominated by the contributions of Zeno and Chrysippus (c. 280–205 BCE); a middle period dominated by Diogenes the Stoic

(c. 150 BCE), Panaetius (c. 183–109 BCE), and Posidonius (c. 135–51 BCE); and the late Stoicism of Roman times, whose main contributors were Seneca the Younger (c. 4 BCE–65 CE), Epictetus (c. 55–135 CE), and, of course, Marcus Aurelius (121–180 CE). Of these, Epictetus likely had the most influence on Aurelius. Epictetus wrote nothing, but some of his teachings survived in notes and discourses transcribed by one of his students. One famous extract attributed to Epictetus that we see reflected in the tone in several of the passages of Aurelius is: "We are disturbed not by events, but by the views which we take of them."

Stoicism was the most successful philosophical movement in the late Greco-Roman world—a success attributable to its capacity to absorb and reconcile ideas from rival branches of philosophy. Ironically, this resilience was responsible in part for the decline of Stoicism as an independent movement, as many of its ideas were in turn absorbed by Christianity and Neoplatonism, movements that coincided with the decline of the Roman world. Stoicism did experience a revival during the Renaissance, and remnants of Stoic thought continue their influence on the modern world. One notable example is the cognitive behavioral technique called Rational Emotive Behavior Therapy (REBT) pioneered by American psychologist Albert Ellis. The basic approach of REBT involves teaching clients how to identify and replace irrational emotive thinking (which is associated with emotional difficulties and depression) with rational thinking.

Stoicism and Religion

The *Meditations* of Marcus Aurelius proclaim that we can be genuinely happy even when surrounded by despair. This is extraordinary. This is not the deluded happiness of denial; Stoics do not bury their heads in the sand. On the contrary, happiness comes about when we engage ourselves fully with the world. Our first duty is always social—to act always in the right way in our relationships to our neighbors, our families, our businesses, our nations, and the world community. Aurelius uses the word *virtue* in describing this duty.

Virtue isn't really a difficult concept. Human beings are in and part of a nature that is good. We ought to mirror this goodness in our moral lives, which means doing the right things in our relationships with others. The language of virtue captures these right actions with words like *justice, courage, temperance,* and *wisdom.* Doing the right thing requires that we possess all of these attributes to some degree. For example, when we help a friend in trouble, we do so because we believe she needs and deserves the help; it is just. We need courage to do this because in helping others we often expose ourselves to risks. The action requires temperance because in helping others we need to deny something that we might want for ourselves. The action is wise because we are able to discern the need and to understand what our friend most requires.

What sets Aurelius and other Stoics apart from the many religious traditions that make similar demands is that the Stoic injunction toward virtue is not grounded in the directive of an external or supernatural authority. It is not the directive of a God revealing intentions for us through Holy Scripture. It is rather the direction of nature, the way the world is. The constant changes and transformations at work in nature result from the inexorable operation of natural laws that never change. What is really important is not the material of which we are made, but the laws that govern our inevitable transformations. Aurelius maintains that the direction to virtue is a logical and rational conclusion any human being will come to after a process of careful self-examination.

English Philosopher John Stuart Mill (1806–1873) was an admirer of Aurelius and wrote compellingly on the *Meditations* in his 1874 posthumously published essay, *The Utility of Religion.* In support of Aurelius's approach to morality, Mill observed that "there is a very real evil consequent on ascribing a supernatural origin to the received maxims of morality. That origin consecrates the whole of them and protects them from being discussed and criticized." Aurelius instead invites us to use discussion and criticism in his approach. In fact, Aurelius lays out a method for us to do precisely that in the *Meditations* (see part 6, "The Method of Stoicism").

The Role of Faith

Another thing that sets Stoicism apart from religious practice is its de-emphasis on the role of faith. For the Stoic, the emphasis shifts from faith to reason and dialogue. The only faith Aurelius requires is a willingness to explore our own nature. Aurelius does not expect us to give uncritical assent to any system founded on unquestioned dogmas.

For the Stoic, every human being is endowed with reason and every human being is capable of understanding what reason demands of us. The Stoic understands reason as the systematic application of logic together with observation, study, research, and discourse. Today we would call the Stoic's approach critical thinking. Reason excludes irrational processes, religious faith, any uncritical acceptance of an authority, or any knowledge based purely on feelings or emotion. This does not imply that Stoicism is meant as an elitist practice, confining its activity to those with special training or academic credentials. Stoic practice is quite the opposite. Every human being is expected to work with reason within whatever capacities for reason nature has bestowed. The Stoic also maintains that whatever capacity for reason each of us does have is precisely what nature wants us to have. Our capacity to be good or virtuous is not a function of intellectual prowess. The Stoic makes no differentiation between a small act of kindness by a simple person and a great act of virtue from a learned sage. Virtue is virtue, and in both cases the result is happiness for the one who is virtuous.

Our Place in the Universe

When we reflect on the natural world, especially on the big picture, we witness the playing out of a cosmic drama governed by natural principles (including the laws of physics, only some of which may be known) that stretch the limits of human imagination. Every atom in every cell of every human being who has ever lived had its genesis in a nuclear fusion of elements within the core of a long-dead star. The long chain of events that led to the births of our sun through the accretion of cosmic debris, our world, our ancestors, and the complex evolution of human life onto our present stage, was brought about by a series of nuclear, gravitational, and electrochemical processes that embrace the entire reach of cosmic space and history. Our protohistory did not begin with our distant relatives, those first organisms on a young Earth somewhere around 3.5 to 4 billion years ago. Those early organisms were themselves distant relatives of much earlier cosmic events that preceded the formation of Earth itself. The universe *is* our home and we are, literally, children of heaven, and that same heaven is mother to us all in far more than an allegorical sense. There are no good reasons to presume that the emergence of life on Earth was a unique or even a rare cosmic event. The physical laws that govern these processes operate in the same way everywhere. Everything and every sentient and nonsentient being in this universe is subject to those laws. The laws are fundamental to existence itself. They cannot be revised or improved or suspended.

Nor is anyone above the law. While it is true that we do not fully understand the law, we are no less subject to its will. As human beings we can and do harness the law—and use it for a purpose, such as harnessing electrochemical processes to create a car battery. But even in doing this we are subject to nature's will. Human beings are also free to oppose the law, as fools sometimes do. But the price we pay in opposing this law is always the same—nature wins. Should we grab the exposed terminals of a fully charged car battery with our bare and sweaty hands, we will experience nature's will. This is the context of the Stoic conception of nature.

What the Stoics inferred from their examination of nature is that nature's law plays itself out in many ways—including the moral plane. There simply seemed to be no reasonable argument for excluding morality—although few other philosophical or religious traditions then (or now) presume that moral teachings can come directly from a study of nature. Yet, for the Stoics, nature revealed what they called "attractions" or "affinities" between objects, which are manifested in many ways: the unified movements of the stars and planets, the herding instincts of animals, the sexual attractions of insects, the flow of a river into the sea.

In turn, these affinities taught the Stoics something about themselves. Bees swarm. Birds of a feather flock together. Fire always rises upward, and rocks fall downward. Each of these demonstrates that like substances have an affinity. So, too, it seemed reasonable that these affinities must extend into the domain of human nature with the natural attraction of all human beings to one another. This natural human affinity, they reasoned, is a synthesis of operations built up from the same laws of nature and makes all humans social by nature.

What Is Reason?

The Stoics inferred from their observations of nature that reason, which is seen only in human beings, is also an expression of a fundamental but even higher law, which they associated with *Logos*—the universal intelligence or highest ruling principle of the universe. The Stoics deduced that the individual human being, as a part of this same nature, must be endowed with at least a part of the same reason that governs the whole. Because the whole is greater than the part, the Stoic concluded that the laws governing the system must override any laws governing the parts—if ever the two conflict. In other words, the welfare of the whole overrides the welfare of the parts. For example, the bee exists for the swarm and the bird for the flock. The survival and happiness of either system requires cooperation between individuals and, when necessary, self-sacrifice. If the death of a part contributes to the welfare of the whole, this death is also what is best for the part; it is "good." This is the same altruistic logic a modern culture applies to human sacrifice in time of war. Soldiers are expected to be ready to die for their country, and willing to do so for the sake of a superior value—the survival of the nation. A cancerous tumor or a gangrenous limb in a single organism will consume the organism unless the tumor is removed or the limb amputated—this "sacrifice" made necessary for the survival of the whole.

The Stoic notion of reason was formulated in the ancient world and based on the laws of nature as understood then. Have discoveries in science invalidated Stoicism? Much has changed, but much remains. The Stoics saw nature as governed by perfect law—a modern thinker cannot say today that the laws of nature are imperfect. The Stoics saw the universe as composed of two material principles or types, active and passive—an equivalent distinction still exists between material particles and the forces of nature. The Stoics saw the universe as an ever-changing dynamic system regulated by principles with parallels to the modern concepts of energy and entropy. The Stoics saw the cosmos as operating through a series of cyclical processes—beginning with a conflagration and followed by an expansion—similar to the modern big bang theory. The ancient Stoics were not aware of relativity or quantum mechanics or black holes or dark matter or cosmic strings or of the true scale of the cosmos. But would this knowledge substantially change what it means to live in accordance with nature? For Aurelius, living in accordance with nature was based on a vision of nature as a dynamic system governed by principles that retain validity. If nature is the template for morality and happiness, a life lived in accordance with the laws of nature as we *now* understand them would look much the same as the life of virtue described by Aurelius.

The Role of Love and Beauty

For the Stoic, the study of nature begins with an inward examination of self. Self-knowledge begins with the understanding of the body and the interrelations of its parts, then extends to an understanding of the mind (or soul) and its interrelations with the larger system of minds that comprises all of humanity. The self-love that emerges in the early stages of these examinations matures into a love of humanity as we identify the operation of our superior trait, our reason, with the operations of nature itself. The affinities seen in nature reveal to us that we as humans are meant to work in concert with other humans. Because the laws underlying these affinities are good and beautiful, we are attracted by them and move with them. The Stoic understands the concept we call love as nothing more than an attraction to beauty. In studying nature rationally, we will uncover this beauty; the more we learn about nature and its unfathomable complexity, the more awe we feel. In discovering beauty, we are drawn to it by the "magnetic" attraction of love. That love grows deeper when, for example, science enables us to discover the great age of a magnificent mountain, the complex structure of a distant galaxy, the strange mating ritual of a tiny spider, or the unexpected chemical properties of a new mineral.

We want somehow to possess the beauty revealed in nature's works because this beauty comes from the operation of perfect laws, and the love we feel for this beauty is an expression of love on the highest plane. The Stoic maintains that this form of love exceeds the beauty and love we may express for anything else—because the beauty and love we feel for these things is a manifestation of the unalloyed and perfect goodness of the laws that make these things the way they are.

When we think like a Stoic and become aware that the beauty we see in nature's perfection comes from the perfect and divine intelligence of the universe, we are as close as we can possibly be to the Stoic conception of the Divine. We are aware, too, that the faculty we are using to contemplate this beauty comes also from this same divine source, and we long to see more and we long to merge with the source. This is how love works, and this is the source of Stoic happiness and joy. On the moral plane, we can merge with the source only by acting in accord with the law of nature—by acting with virtue. In behavioral terms, this means recognizing that the interest of the community comes prior to self-interest. It also means that the operations of reason and the mind take precedence over the interests of the body. In accepting these principles and taking these steps, we draw closer to the real source of good. This is the process that produces the peace and serenity we all seek.

None of this happens automatically. For the Stoic, seeing beauty requires looking for beauty through the faculty of reason. Should we abandon reason (and this is a choice we are free to make), this beauty will forever elude us. We will never follow the law of nature because we have never seen it. We will operate forever in the realm of ignorance, and our attractions (loves) will fixate exclusively on the things we do see at the level of sensation. The objects of our desire will focus exclusively on the material world. In the view of the Stoic, we will then hold the "false" opinion that happiness flows singularly from the satisfaction of bodily pleasures, wealth, material possessions, fame, and the avoidance of pain. But for the Stoic the exclusive pursuit of these things misses the purpose and meaning of existence. It is also irrational—because it represents the failure of reason. It is also contrary to nature—because for the Stoic it is reason that makes us fully human.

The Stoic Position on Pleasure and Pain

For the Stoic, the life of the mind always takes precedence over physical sensations. But this should not imply that pleasure, wealth, fame, or the avoidance of pain is bad or evil. These things in themselves are neither good nor bad. Avoiding pain or seeking pleasure has nothing at all to do with goodness. A Stoic would never characterize any pleasure as good, or any pain as bad. It would be senseless to do that because pleasure and pain are experienced by good persons (those who live in accord with nature) and bad persons (those who live in opposition to nature) alike. But for the Stoic there is a qualitative difference in psychological attitudes toward the experience of pleasure and pain. A Stoic maintains that our attitudes or opinions about pleasure and pain are within our power to regulate. In other words, we can choose how we feel about the sensations that our bodies experience. The internal attitude or opinion a Stoic tries to cultivate here is one of indifference. Yes, a Stoic will prefer pleasure over pain. What human being wouldn't? But a Stoic will never choose pleasure or reject pain at the expense of virtue.

This does not mean that a Stoic is cold and unfeeling—although that is certainly one of the unfortunate stereotypes of the Stoic in the modern world. Nor does this mean that the Stoic can never enjoy pleasure or experience discomfort. The internal attitude of indifference is a strategic choice. The actual sensations of pleasure and pain have nothing to do with reason. They are not rational processes, although they may inform reason and as such can often lead to irrational responses—including addictive behavior (excessive desires for pleasure) or violence (excessive responses to pain). The internalized attitude of indifference toward pleasure and pain is responsible for the undeserved reputation of Stoics as isolated and detached. The opposite is true. All actions of a Stoic are directed toward others, and they are always motivated by love. Stoics understand that their primary duty is social because, at the highest level, every human being is an integral part of a cosmopolitan (broadly based, multiethnic, and multinational) and egalitarian world community. Stoics also feel no contempt for anyone who does not live in harmony with nature's law. They will treat such a person with caution, but also with deep compassion, remembering always that "there, but for *reason*, go I."

Freedom from Harm

The most remarkable consequence of the Stoic orientation toward pleasure and pain is the degree of immunity it offers to the experience of misfortune. All human beings will experience misfortune. No Stoic is immune from disease or death or financial loss or war or terrorism or whatever calamities future climate changes may exact on this world. But the Stoic will maintain that none of these things can touch our governing nature, our capacity for virtue, or our ability to live in accord with nature. It is, after all, our ruling principle that defines what is best in us. This is also the source of our contentment. None of these misfortunes can ever do harm to what is best in us. The Stoic feels pain, but the ruling principle is always immune from harm. The Stoic will also experience personal tragedy. No Stoic wants these things to happen. But the Stoic often reacts to these things in unexpected ways. Pain and loss are never seen as limiting our capacity to be happy, because pleasure, pain, and personal attachments to people or things have little to do with what it means to be human. Stoics may lose a prized possession to a thief and feel distress, but will never feel that this loss is the end of the world, because they will be able to shake it off. They will recognize the anger they may feel as a valid emotional response, but refuse to allow this response to undermine their capacity for reason. Each of the misfortunes mentioned above exists within a world of things, none of which have any bearing on our capacity to be good. We certainly never desire them, but because we are free to determine our attitude toward whatever misfortunes we experience, there is no reason these should ever disturb the tranquility of our soul.

This imperviousness to the more distressing aspects of misfortune is reinforced by the conviction that disasters, be they personal, national, or global, present us with opportunities to set things right—through the exercise of virtue. A Stoic has the capacity to remain free and happy and rational even when living in a sea of despair. This happiness does not come from withdrawal from the world, but from an increased capacity to remain proactive and politically engaged in the affairs of the world.

The Method of Stoicism

Living in accord with nature requires a rational commitment from every human being who decides to follow that path. Following nature demands knowledge of nature, and this requires study. Study activates reason, and reason requires a no-stone-unturned approach to nature that involves research, contemplation, dialogue, and debate, across and through the multiple domains of scientific and human experience, including physics, chemistry, biology, cosmology, sociology, anthropology, history, psychology, literature, philosophy, and epistemology.

Because every human being is capable of reason, every human being is capable of participation at some level in this ongoing human project. The so-called methods of science will be important in this task, but science is only one of the ways whereby human beings might come to know nature. The task extends beyond the academic pursuit of knowledge and must acknowledge that ways of knowing the world may extend beyond multidisciplinarian approaches to knowledge. The process needs to be receptive to alternative ways of knowing. The goal also extends past a pursuit of knowledge for its own sake. The focus is moral. For the Stoic, the law of nature is the template for virtue—for acting rightly in the world. Doing the right thing requires accurate understanding of natural law and is fostered by the light of reason.

The Practical Benefits of Stoicism

You do not need to buy into Stoicism in order to get something useful from reading this book. You certainly do not need to become a Stoic to reflect on its basic principles. What this book will do is help you address a big question. How should you live your life? You may not like or agree with the answers Aurelius offers, but it is hard to reject the way he approaches the question. The approach he uses rests on an argument; the argument rests on observable phenomena; the phenomena are arranged systematically into a set of principles; the principles imply consequences. It's an appealing framework anyone can follow, and it produces stunning results.

Aurelius begins by dividing the world into two parts: one active and one passive. That division was an informed opinion; it wasn't just a random guess. It was the way the universe appeared to be in the eyes of the ancient world. It was based on physics and it made sense. Has the universe changed so much that divisions like these are no longer useful? Is there a better starting point than this? Feel free to ask those sorts of questions when reading these meditations. Aurelius expects you to.

The dichotomy Aurelius saw in nature produced three fundamental principles: human beings are social; the intellectual is superior to the physical; and because the mind is governed by perfect law, it is immune from external harm. What principles would you offer based on whatever divisions you might propose? What consequences would your principles imply? What implications would your derived principles have on how you should live your life? Raise these questions as you read through these chapters, run them past your ruling principle, use reason as best you can, and challenge Aurelius. Take a deep breath, clear your mind of worry, then retire (as Aurelius invites you to do) into this mind, gracefully. Enjoy the journey!

A Note on the Translation

The translation I use in this text is based on *Thoughts of Marcus Aurelius* (1862) by the British classical scholar George Long from its republished version as *The Meditations of Marcus Aurelius* (1900–1914).[1] Long held professorships in Greek and Latin in Britain (University of London) and the United States (University of Virginia) and was editor of *Bibliotheca Classica* (1851–1862), an important series of classical works with English commentaries.

In praising the George Long translation of Aurelius, Matthew Arnold said that Long had succeeded in "faithfully" reproducing his thoughts. Interestingly, Arnold observed that Long's translation was actually "incomparably more valuable" than the original Greek manuscript. The Greek used by Aurelius was "crabbed," by which Arnold meant obscure or hard to understand. Greek was a foreign tongue for Aurelius; his native language was Latin. Then, as was the case for many centuries after Aurelius, Greek was the accepted language for scholars, but the technical Greek Aurelius used tended to mask the poetic charm and personal qualities of its author. Arnold believed that Long succeeded in bringing to his translation the quality of language and expression characteristic of the man himself. As to the accuracy of the translation, Arnold noted that "Mr. Long's reputation as a scholar is a sufficient guarantee of the general fidelity and accuracy." Long succeeded in bringing Aurelius back into the world as a man "engaged in the current of contemporary life and action." Arnold goes on to say that Long "treats this truly modern striver and thinker [Aurelius] not as a Classical Dictionary hero but as a present source from which to draw 'example of life, and instruction of manners.'"

Although Long's translation of the *Meditations* certainly possesses the "fidelity and accuracy" that Arnold asserts, it was done in the late nineteenth century using conventions and language in vogue during those Victorian times, including Long's habit of assuming the masculine form of a pronoun whenever a gender assignment was called for. The intrusion of these devices and presumptions into the original translation colors and biases Aurelius's meanings in uncomfortable ways. I have taken the liberty of modernizing these anachronistic conventions (and words) in a way that I trust does no disservice to the work, or to the intention, of Marcus Aurelius.

For example, in one passage Long's original language, "Remember that to change thy opinion and to follow him who corrects thy error is as consistent with freedom as it is to persist in thy error," becomes, "Remember that to change your opinion and to follow whoever corrects your error is as consistent with freedom as it is to persist in your error." In a similar fashion, "He who acts unjustly acts impiously" becomes, "The person who acts unjustly acts profanely (impiously)." In the same spirit, the phrase "that thou mayest know whether he has acted ignorantly or with knowledge, and that thou mayest also consider that his ruling faculty is akin to thine" reemerges as "that you may know whether she has acted ignorantly or with knowledge, and that you may also consider that her ruling faculty is akin to yours."

A second and important difference between Long's translation and this rendering is the omission of most of Long's translated references to God. I've done this in a dozen or so instances, not to wring God out of the universe, but to bring some consistency to those textual references to God. Aurelius does sometimes refer to the "ruling intelligence of the universe" as God. In one place he even refers to Zeus in a similar context. But this same ruling intelligence is also referred to interchangeably as "universal reason" or "*Logos*" or "the ruling principle" or "nature" or even "reason."

Translating this idea—which for Aurelius does admittedly express qualities he calls divine—as "God" can be confusing. That word is charged with preprogrammed meanings for most of us. We tend to think of and associate the word *God* and its use in terms of our own experiences. The God of Stoicism *is* the active principle *in* and *of* nature. This God never expresses herself as a personal being, although the pronoun substituting for nature is always feminine—this I have retained. This Stoic God never speaks or reveals herself in any way—other than as a ruling principle or law. If we were to refer to this concept as God we would need also to refer to human beings as gods, too—the same ruling intelligence sometimes referred to as God is also *in* and a part of each of us as the essential defining ingredient of our humanness. The Stoic God is pantheistic and corporeal. It is part of the material word, and is the active material in the cosmos. As such, this God is knowable using the methods and principles of physics. This means that to a Stoic physicist (if any still remain) God is both an observable and a measurable property of the universe. Rendering this extraordinary idea as God inserts unnecessary confusions into the *Meditations.*

Thus, Long's rendition of the phrase; "These two things are common both to the soul of God and to the soul of man" becomes; "These two things are held in common in nature, and in the intelligence of every rational being." In another place; "What a power man has to do nothing except what God will approve, and to accept all that God may give him" becomes; "What power we have! To do nothing except what the perfect ruling intelligence expects, and to accept all that nature provides." And finally; "God has allowed this to no other part, after it has been separated and cut asunder, to come together again," reemerges as; "The ruling intelligence has allowed this to no other part after it has been separated and cut asunder, to come together again."

1 □ The Promise
of Stoicism

1 For Aurelius, personal opinion is one of the powers that we can control independently without interference from others. Aurelius often uses the concept of opinion when referring to things such as wealth, fame, pleasure, or pain. Many people seek pleasure or avoid pain because they hold the opinion that these things are best for them in life, or in the case of pain, the worst. But as we will see in the *Meditations*, the things that Aurelius believes are really good (or bad) have nothing to do with pleasure or pain.

2 A promontory is a peninsula that acts as a natural breakwater around the edges of a bay. The waters surrounding a ship sailing into a bay become calmer as the promontory widens.

3 The direction of this meditation is more toward removing an opinion than developing one. The first step in developing a serene outlook in life is to get rid of false opinions about things we cannot control. This is also something that we have the power to control. The next step is to develop new opinions about the things that truly are in our interest, once we are in this "waveless bay."

4 No single authority has a corner on truth or absolute wisdom. Aurelius encourages us to always be open to new opinions and to feel free to change our opinion. It is clear from the passage that Aurelius regards some people as closer to the truth than others. He believes such people are in a better position to correct error. These sages, as they are sometimes called, may be closer to truth than others because they have questioned more thoroughly.

☐ The Power of Opinion

Consider that everything is opinion,[1] and opinion is in your power. Take away then, when you choose, your opinion, and like a mariner, who has doubled the promontory,[2] you will find calm, everything stable, and a waveless bay.[3]

—XII:22

Remember that to change your opinion and to follow whoever corrects your error is as consistent with freedom as it is to persist in your error....[4]

—VIII:16

5 The meditative exercise Aurelius advocates is a voyage into the mind—the locus of our rationality. Reason is what makes us fully human. As mentioned in the Introduction, reason, or *Logos,* is the active principle in nature. Reason is a material substance bearing properties that in some ways seem to forecast the forces and fields of modern physics. While reason behaves in providential ways at the cosmic scale, it is not a transcendent entity, as is, for example, the God of the Judeo-Christian tradition. What is important here is that individual human reason comes from cosmic reason. We are connected through this reason to the universe as a whole and connected to every other human being through our common origin in reason. Because we share this rational principle with every other rational creature in the world, this seemingly solitary internal withdrawal is—ironically—a social act.

6 In a single world community of rational individual souls (the soul is the seat of human reason) sharing a common world soul (*Logos*), any sort of unjust activity by one is an irrational assault on every member of the human race. Really, this is an act of war against the unity of the whole, because we are tethered to each other through reason.

7 This is the tranquility and serenity derived from cooperative peace.

Retire into yourself.[5] The rational principle which rules our lives has this nature—it is content with itself when it does what is just,[6] and so secures tranquility.[7]

—VII:28

8 The remote country home is an example of the perfect retreat or idyllic oasis in a culture where happiness is secured through wealth and property. Aurelius counters with an entirely different meaning for retreat.

9 Aurelius never demands ascetic practices. There's no need to surrender material possessions, but these will become increasingly irrelevant once we discover where true serenity lies.

10 The Stoic concept of the soul is associated with *Logos*. Although this soul is materialistic and integrated with the body (the passive principle in nature), it is immune from external attack. A falling egg—a material substance comprising the passive principle of nature—may be destroyed by gravity, an active principle. But the active principle is immune to the falling egg.

11 Plato (387–347 BCE) modeled the human mind or soul (*psyche*) as having three divisions: desiring, spirited, and reasoning. These three parts correspond to appetite, emotion, and intellect. In his *Republic,* Plato argues that personal justice (good ordering of the mind) occurs when the three parts of the soul are properly educated. Philosophy, for example, is proper for the reasoning part of the soul, while music is best for the spirited part of the soul, and physical education (gymnastics being best) is important for the education of the desiring part. A person is just when the reasoning part of the soul takes precedence over spirit or desire. In other words, our emotions and our physical desires should always be mediated by reason.

12 Aurelius will refer to these principles in more detail later. In substance, there are three: human beings are primarily social; we must never yield priority to the demands of the body; and the mind is where our true nature lies. The human mind, when properly conditioned, is always immune from error.

13 The principles Aurelius uses to cleanse the soul are addressed in the Introduction and in more detail in part 6, "The Method of Stoicism," and part 8, "The Practice of Stoicism."

We seek retreats for ourselves, houses in the country, sea-shores, and mountains; and you too are disposed to desire such things very much.[8] But this is altogether a mark of the most common sort of person, for it is in your power whenever you shall choose to retire into yourself.[9] For nowhere either with more quiet or more freedom from trouble do you retire than into your own soul,[10] particularly when you have within you such thoughts that by looking into them you are immediately in perfect tranquility; and I affirm that tranquility is nothing else than the good ordering of the mind.[11] Constantly then give to yourself this retreat, and renew yourself; and let your principles[12] be brief and fundamental, which, as soon as you shall refer to them, will be sufficient to cleanse the soul completely, and to send you back free from all discontent with the things to which you return.[13]

—IV:3

14 Intelligence, or critical thinking (see part 6, "The Method of Stoicism"), demonstrates that pleasure and pain are neither good nor bad, because good and bad people alike share these things. When we perceive pleasure (love of excess) or avoid pain (laziness, for example) as desirable and good, we miss opportunities to do real good through the exercise of virtue (sincerity, benevolence, frankness, and generosity). The virtues are our only real sources of happiness, and the only things that are fully under our control. When we understand the true nature of goodness, it is these activities that will make us happy.

15 Aurelius acknowledges that, in spite of best intentions, we are human and subject to the whims of the body and distractions of the mind. Aurelius frequently used self-deprecation as a method of reproach and correction. This passage serves as a reminder that while there are things we cannot control, the virtues are always within our power.

16 Sometimes we sense that life has no meaning. We may express the malaise we feel as hopelessness and despair. These feelings of purposelessness may arise from personal misfortune, broken dreams, or the loss of a loved one. They may also arise when surrounded by the trappings of material success, wealth, or fame. We long for a simpler time, the restoration of lost innocence, or simpler values.

It is in these moments that we need to recover our lives. The solution Aurelius offers focuses on the root cause of malaise. These feelings of desperation occur when we substitute things we once valued with the counterfeit lure of material pleasures. For Aurelius, this solution does not work, and any opinion that it does is false. The good news is that we can eradicate malaise—not by longing for more comfort or less pain, but by adjusting our attitudes and looking at the world as we did in simpler times. On its own, this meditation offers nothing more than a possibility. Learning how to do this requires a program of action, a method, and a degree of faith. Several strategies for achieving this are reviewed in part 6, "The Method of Stoicism."

Show to others those qualities, which are altogether in your power. These are sincerity, gravity, endurance of labor, aversion to pleasure, contentment with what you have and with a very few things, benevolence, frankness, no love of excess, and generosity of spirit.[14] Do you not see how many qualities you are immediately able to exhibit, in which there is no excuse of natural incapacity and unfitness, and yet you still remain voluntarily below the mark? Or are you compelled through being defectively furnished by nature to murmur, and to be stingy, and to flatter, and to find fault with your poor body, and to try to please people, and to make great display, and to be so restless in your mind?[15]

—V:5

You have the power to recover your life. To do so you need to look at things as you once did.[16]

—VII:2

17 The things we can control include our opinions, which we are free to reject if they are false. We can do this when we "examine each thing closely." We can also eliminate desire, by "letting nothing bad into this soul." These powers are available to us if we have made a decision to live according to nature. That decision triggers the examination of nature that allows us to reject the thoughts that lie outside of nature. In doing these things we will be free of anxiety.

18 The "natural unity" refers here to the ruling principle of nature.

19 This passage reflects the Stoic conception of sin and its forgiveness. It bears some similarity to the biblical parable of the return of the prodigal son told in Luke 15:11–32. In the story, a wasteful son returns home to the welcoming and forgiving arms of his father, evoking the jealousy of his older brother. In this Aurelian parallel of that story, an infinitely kind and forgiving nature (identified always as feminine and mothering by Aurelius) plays the role of the forgiving father in the biblical parable.

Nature never prevents people who have abandoned their principles from returning to the fold. Sin, in Stoic terms, is any action contrary to nature. Self-serving behavior, such as valuing pleasure over generosity, is one example of sin. Aurelius tells us that these things are usually a consequence of ignorance rather than willful malice. Actions contrary to nature are inherently bad (or unsocial) because they disconnect us from the social unity of the cosmos through which we are all socially and politically connected in our common origin in reason. Forgiveness, in the Stoic scheme, actually means self-forgiveness—something Stoics need to do when they knowingly act contrary to nature. Stoics do not normally feel the need to forgive sin in others, because it is generally presumed that those acts are done out of ignorance. The ignorance we observe in others triggers a duty to guide the sinner away from error. Living a life according to nature is therefore an informed choice and is always completely within our power. It is never dependent upon the mercy of the father or mother.

Remember these powers you have from nature: to reject false thinking; to limit desire; to be free from anxiety; to let nothing bad into this soul. Examine each thing closely and determine its real nature; and make use of each thing according to its value.[17]

—VIII:29

If you should ever see a hand cut off, or a foot, or a head, lying anywhere apart from the rest of the body, this is what you make of yourself, if you are not content with what happens, or if you separate yourself from others, or do anything unsocial. Suppose that you have detached yourself from the natural unity[18]—for you were made by nature a part, but now you have cut yourself off. Yet even here there is this beautiful provision that it is in your power to become whole again. The ruling intelligence has allowed this to no other part after it has been separated and cut asunder, to come together again. But consider the kindness with which nature distinguishes humanity, for nature has put it in our power not to be separated at all from the universal; and when we have been separated, nature allows us to return and to be united and to resume our place as a part.[19]

—VIII:34

20 Human beings have the same kinds of powers as the governing intelligence of the universe. But there is a difference in degree; as rational agents, we are a part of the whole. These powers include opinion, desire, and action. As individual agents, each of these powers is limited to the confines of our personal spheres of action; the same powers reside in the universal intelligence, but those powers have influence over everyone.

21 A falling apple cannot oppose, or hinder, the law of gravity; the concept is irrational. Even if we throw the apple into the air, the law of gravity works in harmony with the law of energy conservation (both are according to nature), and the apple eventually resumes its downward fall. Nothing in nature has the capacity to oppose these laws. All human technologies must also work within these constraints. When nature is opposed (such as when pigs try to fly), this opposition is always assimilated back into itself. Apples, of course, never leap into the sky, and pigs do not fly. Unlike apples and pigs, though, humans, as rational agents, are free to attempt to oppose the universal law of reason—a complex law, surely, but no less a law than the simpler laws of nature. But such opposition is as irrational and futile as opposing the laws of physics. Alternately, we have the power to cooperate with and harness nature to achieve our purposes—insofar as our purposes conform to nature. For example, in understanding the natural principles of lift, we are able to construct machines that will fly.

In the moral sphere we do have the freedom of referring all actions to ourselves—for example, choosing personal pleasure over virtue as our path to happiness. To the Stoic, however, this choice opposes natural law because nature is social—the law of nature directs us to focus our activities outwardly toward others. In the end, this sort of opposition is self-defeating. We will never find real happiness or experience invincibility in this way; in living this way, we will have done nothing to advance nature's design. When life is over, we will be absorbed back into, and recycled by, the nature that produced us in the beginning.

The nature of the universal has given to every human being all the rational powers that it has. So too we have received from the universal the power of invincibility.[20] For the universal nature converts and fixes in its predestined place everything which opposes it, and makes such things a part of itself. So also has the rational human mind the power to transform every hindrance into an advantage and to use this for such purposes as it may have designed.[21]

—VIII:35

22   The apparent paradox between so-called free will and Stoic destiny is sometimes compared to a flowing river (destiny) with its numerous eddies (free will). The waters may take a circuitous route and even reverse directions, but at the end of the day the river does flow into the sea. In any case, the free actions of others can never harm our essential nature, our capacity for reason. A neighbor can injure our bodies or our breath and flesh, but can never impair our ability to reason.

23   Humans are by nature social, but we are also all independent agents in the world. In other words, we have free will.

24   Wickedness, sin, evil, and badness are always presumed to arise from ignorance. For this reason, the Stoic always views the misdeeds of a neighbor with compassion. A neighbor can never harm our ruling power with his transgressions, because the ruling power is always invincible from harm. Hence, the actions of a neighbor should never be cause for revenge.

25   It is not necessary to become overly mechanical in describing Stoic physics. It's enough to recall that material substance is passive matter. As understood from evidence available to the ancient world, normal materials are an amalgam of some combination of earth, air, water, or fire. Today we know normal matter as chemical combinations or mixtures of one or more of the ninety-two naturally occurring elements in the periodic table. For the ancient Stoic, the soul is also material (or corporeal) but formed from active matter, a finer substance that the Stoics presumed was unaffected by passive matter. In some ways, the active matter of ancient Stoic physics manifests properties similar to the force fields of modern physics. So, on one level, the Stoics seemed to imagine mental activity as a complex process mediated through electrochemical mechanisms. On another level, the Stoics recognized that mental activity had a capacity also to transcend space and time.

To my own free will, the free will of my neighbor is just as indifferent as his poor breath and flesh.[22] For though we are made especially for the sake of one another, still the ruling power in each of us has its own office.[23] If this were not so, my neighbor's wickedness would be my harm. Nature has not willed that my unhappiness should depend on another.[24]

—VIII:56

Things themselves cannot touch the soul, not in the least degree—nor have they admission to the soul, nor can they turn or move the soul. The soul turns and moves itself alone. And whatever judgments the soul may think proper to make, those it makes for itself about the things which present themselves to the soul.[25]

—V:19

26   The intelligence Aurelius reflects on in this beautiful passage touches on the Stoic concept of divine purpose and meaning; the language brushes up against the concept of deity. It may be helpful to understand that modern physicists who search for Grand Unified Theories (GUTs) and Theories of Everything (TOEs) are also seeking a single thread that would tie one-to-all and all-to-one, through a unification of the various force fields of physics.

It's hard to avoid the temptation of assigning the name "God" to this intelligence. But when the Stoic does, the God that results is substantially different from the God of many religious traditions. This God is in nature, not above. This God is also finite, material, and—unlike the Judeo-Christian deity—forever tethered to and part of our personal psyche through the reason it shares with all of us.

If it does that for which it has been made, every instrument, tool, and vessel is fitted for its task, and yet the creator who made it is not there. But in the things which are bound together by nature, there is within and there abides in these the power which made them; wherefore the more is it fit to respect this power, and to think, that, if you live and act according to its will, everything in you is in conformity to intelligence. And thus also in the universe the things which belong to it are in conformity to intelligence.[26]

—VI:40

1 Stoics do not hold that money is the root of all evil. Wealth in and of itself is neither a bad thing nor a good thing. The Stoic attitude toward fame and fortune is one of indifference because neither can bring genuine happiness—only virtue does that. That said, wealth or prosperity may be preferred over poverty, but wealth is always rejected if its possession prevents us from the pursuit of virtue, or promotes arrogance. I explore the concept of virtue more closely in part 5, "Stoicism and the Mind."

2 This touch of sardonic humor illustrates Aurelius's disdain for empty posthumous reputation. It is ironic that this emperor's fame still shines nearly two millennia after his death.

3 The other person's "activity" Aurelius refers to here is the hero-worshipping attitude of admirers. Aurelius finds this ridiculous. If you are admired, how does that make you good? Such admiration has nothing to do with your personal actions. Only our own actions can be good. These must also be the right kinds of actions—actions within our power—and done for the benefit of others.

4 The "sensations" Aurelius refers to are the feelings experienced by those who worship others. But people who worship others are really only indulging in a form of pleasure with their misplaced adoration. But pleasure, Aurelius reminds us, is not a good. Famous people (for example, rock stars) may also feel good sensations in knowing that they are adored, but these are, again, nothing other than misplaced pleasures. These do not make them good people.

5 "Understanding" is an opinion acquired through the use of reason. This sort of opinion can lead to the exercise of virtue—through individual action—and this is a personal good. This is also the only way we may secure personal happiness.

☐ Fame and Fortune as False Values

Receive wealth or prosperity without arrogance; and be ready to let it go.[1]

—VIII:33

See that you live in this present time and secure this for yourself. But do those who instead pursue posthumous fame not consider that the people of after time will be exactly such as these whom they cannot bear now? And both are mortal. And what is it in any way to you if these people who are not yet born utter this or that sound, or have this or that opinion about you?[2]

—VIII:44

Whoever loves fame considers another's activity to be a personal good;[3] and personal sensations are considered good to whoever loves pleasure;[4] but the person who has understanding, considers individual action to be a personal good.[5]

—VI:51

1 The Stoic concept of philosophy refers simply to the idea of desiring and loving truth. Anyone who behaves in the right way is a philosopher.

2 How we seem to others (our social reputation) is a form of fame. Aurelius views this sort of pleasure as meaningless. The fear of a bad reputation can restrict us from doing the right things—particularly when they are unpopular. But this is exactly what nature wills.

3 If you have already seen in your "wanderings" that fancy arguments or conversations (syllogisms) or money or fame or pleasures do not yield happiness, then do what nature wills, and then you will discover peace.

4 "Your nature requires" virtuous acts—these are the only things that promote happiness because these are according to nature. This means acting altruistically. We will never do this if we do not understand what virtue requires.

5 In the language of Stoics, an "affect" is the conscious subjective aspect of a feeling (such as a sexual attraction toward a stranger). A rational act is guided by reason and never controlled by raw emotion; an irrational act is guided exclusively by feelings. As human beings, affects cannot be avoided. However, the character of an affect is determined by whether we give assent to (yield and act on) the impression that produces the feeling.

If I am hungry and smell food, I will desire the food based on my sense impressions. This is the affect. But if I am in the company of someone who is starving, my reason will direct me to give the food to her. In doing this, I deny giving assent to the desire, and instead act virtuously.

6 The virtues are good in and of themselves, and being virtuous is both necessary and sufficient for happiness. These principles come from understanding the differences between virtue and vice, or from understanding the differences between living according to nature and living contrary to nature.

☐ The Promise of Happiness

This reflection also tends to the removal of the desire of empty fame, that it is no longer in your power to have lived the whole of your life, or at least your life from your youth upwards, like a philosopher; but both to many others and to yourself it is plain that you are far from philosophy. You have fallen into disorder then, so that it is no longer easy for you to get the reputation of a philosopher; and your plan of life also opposes it.[1] If then you have truly seen where the matter lies, throw away the thought, *How you shall seem to others,* and be content if you shall live the rest of your life as your nature wills.[2] Observe then what it wills, and let nothing else distract you; for you have had experience of many wanderings without having found happiness anywhere, not in syllogisms, nor in wealth, nor in reputation, nor in enjoyment, nor anywhere.[3] *Where then is happiness?* In doing what your nature requires.[4] *How then shall a human being do this?* Happiness in the principles from which come your affects and your acts.[5] *What principles are these?* Those which relate to good and bad—the belief that there is nothing good for you, which does not make you just, temperate, humane, free—and that there is nothing bad for you that does not do the contrary to what has been mentioned.[6]

—VIII:1

7 This passage is the key to Stoical serenity and the popular understanding of Stoic behavior. We are bombarded by impressions. Every impression we receive produces a sensation or feeling—many of which are troublesome, unsuitable, or inappropriate. If we give assent to these impressions we are likely to act in troublesome, unsuitable, or inappropriate ways. However, if we genuinely refuse to give assent to impressions, we will remain tranquil. The only way we will ever refuse to give assent is by making reference to and believing in moral principles. For the Stoic, the choice is informed by understanding that some things are bad not because of some written law or social convention, but because we have studied nature and we truly know the difference between what is good and what is bad.

8 This gentle passage is disarming in the universality of its appeal. There is nothing elitist about Stoicism. The philosophy is accessible to anyone who will open his or her mind to the voice of nature. The reward is an authentic and joyful life free of pretense and posturing.

How easy it is to repel and to wipe away every impression which is troublesome or unsuitable, and immediately to be in all tranquility.[7]

—V:2

Always remember this. Nature has not so mixed intelligence and body that you may easily separate the two. It is quite possible to be wise but not regarded so. Remember that very little indeed is necessary to live a happy life. Do you despair of appearing refined or educated? This is irrelevant. These will never prevent you from being free and modest and social and obedient to nature.[8]

—VII:67

1 This chilling meditation warns those whose lives revolve around money, fame, material possessions, or pleasure. Such things are worthless—in choosing these, our life has no value. This admonition is as close as Aurelius comes to fire and brimstone. There is no afterlife in the Stoic scheme: no heaven or hell. All that we have in our fleeting encounter with existence is the one opportunity to act within nature's design. If we reject this, the joys of fidelity, modesty, justice, and truth—and the serenity these promise—elude us forever.

Hell for the Stoic is a life of anxiety and despair—a self-willed punishment. Such a life will reflect the spirit of the poem "The Lay of the Last Minstral" by Sir Walter Scott (1771–1832). In passing, such a person "shall go down—to the vile dust from whence he sprung, unwept, unhonored, and unsung."

2 "These things only" are the basic terms in our contract with nature. This could serve also as a business mission statement, the preface to a national constitution, a marriage contract, or simply a personal code of conduct: Carry out all of our affairs in a spirit of justice; never put personal gain before social duty; all that happens to us, for good or ill, is as it should be, and is always what is best for the world.

Such a life is a life of virtue and is the best that any life can be. When we do these things, we will know serenity and we will know joy. We will be happy and we will be free. When such a life is over, it is over. We will have fulfilled our duty to the universe. We will have lived our life according to nature. Our life will have been as it was meant to be, and our life will have been our reward.

☐ A Contract with Nature

Soon, very soon, you will be ashes, or a skeleton, and either a name or not even a name; but name is sound and echo. And the things that are much valued in life are empty and rotten and trifling, and like little dogs biting one another, and little children quarrelling, laughing, and then straightaway weeping. But fidelity and modesty and justice and truth have fled.[1]

—V:33

What then is that about which we ought to employ our serious efforts? These things only, thoughts just, and acts social, and words which never lie, and a disposition which gladly accepts all that happens as necessary, as usual, as flowing from a principle and source of the same kind.[2]

—IV:33

1 Life evolves. Existence is change—the product of a constant flow and intermingling between the two material principles of nature. The rational or active principle of nature is itself always in constant flux. When reason is not engaged we do nothing more than simply exist, but this is contrary to nature. The active principle of nature is never still. Because our reason comes from this active principle, we too need to act. The idea of a continual renewal between opposing principles has parallels in the Taoist principles of yin (passive) and yang (active), which are in continual movement and dynamic tension.

2 In his *Almagest,* the Greek astronomer Claudius Ptolemy (c. 85–c. 165 CE) described the earth "as a point" in relation to the stars. Modern readers may be surprised that the ancient world was aware that space was vast. They did not conceive of the immeasurably large distances we understand the cosmos to be today, yet the ancients were no less in awe of the heavens than we are now.

Aurelius also understood that the earth was a sphere with dimensions close to those we know now. The Greek astronomer Eratosthenes (276–194 BCE) calculated the size of the earth more than four hundred years before Aurelius lived. He did this by using simple geometry to measure the angle of a shadow cast by a vertical pole in Alexandria, Egypt. The measurement was made at noon on the same day the sun was directly overhead at Syene at the First Cataract (Aswan in modern Upper Egypt—about 500 miles due south). His value for the circumference was very close to the modern value of 24,900 miles. This value would make Earth seem very large to Aurelius, especially in relation to the scale of a human being.

The enormous scale of the cosmos in comparison to the size of Earth is one of those facts of nature that informs the mind of the Stoic. Living in the world and living according to nature requires living within this awareness. For Aurelius, the measure of humanity is nothing in comparison to the earth, and less than nothing in comparison to the universe. A modern Stoic could say no more or no less than this. The

(continued on page 28)

☐ Time, Motion, Cosmology, and Evolution

It is no evil for things to undergo change, and no good for things to subsist in consequence of change.[1]

—IV:42

Short-lived are both the praiser and the praised, and the rememberer and the remembered: and all this in a nook of this part of the world; and not even here do all agree, no, not any one with himself: and the whole earth too is a point.[2]

—VIII:21

"praiser and the praised" are short-lived—so too "the rememberer and the remembered"—as it was then, so it is now. Cosmic scale is humbling, and humility is one example of a virtue that the knowledge of nature can inspire.

3 The notion that the more things change, the more they stay the same, permeates Aurelius's thinking. That belief is rooted in the Stoic cosmic theory that the universe undergoes endless cyclic renewals. In these cycles, the universe begins with a birth in fire, followed by an active, ever-changing development period. This sequence is repeated in an endless chain. A modern cosmic theory pioneered by Paul Steinhardt at Princeton University and Neil Turok at the University of Cambridge borrows the Greek word *ekpyrotic* (born out of fire) for their description of a cyclic model of the universe comprising an endless sequence of cosmic events that begin with a bang and end with a crunch (Paul J. Steinhardt, and Neil Turok, *Science*, vol. 296, May 24, 2002, p. 1439). This cosmic model, also called the "brane" theory, attempts to reconcile some of the philosophical objections of the so-called big bang, which by many accounts sees the universe as ever-expanding and never ending. But—what happened before the big bang? Was everything created out of nothing? How? Questions like these are unnecessary with the *ekpyrotic* and similar competing models.

Cosmologies have a profound effect on how we think. The idea, for example, that history is always "going forward" is a refrain in the language of politicians. Like the discussion on cosmic scale in the previous note, the prevalent cosmological model of the universe in any era is one of those facts that determines what living according to nature means, and permeates both Stoic and modern thought. In contrast, the series of universes envisioned by the ancient Stoic seemed to discourage thinking about history as a series of progressive steps, with each stage an improvement on the one it followed. The movement of history—and more so science—in the modern world is generally viewed as forward. Historical movement in the ancient world was regarded in a more cyclical fashion: rests followed by movements in endlessly repeated cycles.

All things are the same, familiar in experience, and ephemeral in time, and worthless in the matter. Everything now is just as it was in the time of those whom we have buried.[3]

—IX:14

4 Aurelius enjoyed offering practical examples of change. Life for Aurelius seemed to follow a predetermined path programmed by cosmic inevitability.

Today, with some qualifications, the fact that everything changes, ages, and dies might be explained as a consequence of the thermodynamic law of entropy. Entropy is a measure of the ever-increasing amount of energy *unavailable* for doing useful things. Very simply put, entropy in a so-called closed system, such as the human body, increases over the long term. Essentially, we wind down. From a Stoic perspective, fighting or masking these changes is contrary to the laws of nature, and stands in opposition to virtue, beauty, and the good. Aurelius seems to draw on some intuitive awareness of this idea to refute those who seek immortality, not only in physical terms but also through the acquisition of reputation or fame. The fact that nothing lasts—even the memory of our name—could be attributed to the action of the concept of entropy, but on a larger scale.

5 Aurelius expresses an awareness that Earth has changed, and will continue so forever. If the modern estimate of the age of the earth—more than 4.5 billion years—was compressed into 24 hours, recorded human history (50,000 years) would occupy the final second. If Aurelius had known this, it is unlikely that he would have changed his language. The age of the earth would still seem "soon" to Aurelius, especially when contrasted with the eternity of cosmic cycles, as envisioned in Stoic cosmology.

Is anyone afraid of change? What can take place without change? What then is more pleasing or more suitable to the universal nature? And can you take a heated bath unless the firewood undergoes a change? And can you be nourished, unless the food undergoes a change? And can anything else that is useful be accomplished without change? Do you not see then that for yourself also to change is just the same, and equally necessary for the universal nature?[4]

—VII:18

Soon will the earth cover us all: then the earth, too, will change, and the things also which result from change will continue to change forever, and these again forever. For if you reflect on the changes and transformations which follow one another like wave after wave and their rapidity, you will despise everything which is perishable.[5]

—IX:28

6 Aurelius addresses motion and change using the analogy of breath. "The whole respiratory power" is an allusion to *Logos*, the active principle of nature from which our power of reason is derived. We draw in our power from *Logos* at birth; we return it at death. When we attach inordinate value to wealth, possessions, pleasures, or fame, we attempt to hold onto those things as if they would remain forever. But in doing this we are attaching value to and developing pride in things that come and go like one of the "sparrows that fly by." When we do this, we miss the truth about nature's processes—that everything is in motion and flux. To live in accord with this law of nature we, too, must release our pride and act with nature, and die in nature.

Some things are hurrying into existence, and others are hurrying out of it; and of that which is coming into existence, part is already extinguished. Motions and changes are continually renewing the world, just as the uninterrupted course of time is always renewing the infinite duration of ages. In this flowing stream then, on which there is no abiding, what is there of the things which hurry by on which I would set a high price? It would be just as if I should fall in love with one of the sparrows that fly by, but it has already passed out of sight. Something of this kind is the very life of everyone, like the exhalation of the blood and the respiration of the air. For such as it is to have once drawn in the air and to have given it back, which we do every moment, just the same is it with the whole respiratory power, which you did receive at your birth yesterday and the day before, to give it back to the element from which you did first draw it.[6]

—VI:15

1 For Aurelius, fate and destiny are programmed into the universe. Nature's flow is inexorable. Accept your destiny and you will be happy. Reject your destiny and you will be miserable. The proverb best capturing this Stoic sentiment is "What happens, happens for the best." The wisdom behind the sentiment is captured in the famous phrase "the universe is unfolding as it should," from the 1827 prose poem "The Desiderata of Happiness" by American writer Max Ehrmann (1872–1945). The influence of Stoicism seems apparent in that poem's most famous passage: "And whether or not it is clear to you, no doubt the universe is unfolding as it should. Therefore be at peace with God, whatever you conceive Him to be. And whatever your labors and aspirations, in the noisy confusion of life, keep peace in your soul. With all its sham, drudgery, and broken dreams, it is still a beautiful world. Be cheerful. Strive to be happy."

✦ The discoveries of modern physics in the twentieth century have shaken the notions of causality that lay at the foundation of the early Stoic worldview about fate and destiny. The fact that physical events at the subatomic level proceed in indeterminate ways would likely come as a shock to Aurelius. The ancient Stoic believed that all events in the future will be the consequences of an unbroken chain of antecedent events. We now know this is not possible. Quantum mechanics demonstrates that the outcomes of future physical events can only be expressed as probabilities. In other words, the world does *not* evolve fatefully along a predetermined path.

Still, even in modern physics, future events do not necessarily come as a complete surprise. The probabilities of quantum mechanics do tell us something about the way nature behaves. Stoics were not fond of proclaiming dogmatic truths about nature, beyond enunciating fundamental principles. The mandate of the Stoic was simple: our duty is to live according to nature and its laws, whatever they may be. Our duty then, as now, is to discover those laws.

☐ Fate and Destiny

That is for the good of each thing, which the universal nature brings to each. And it is for its good at the time when nature brings it.[1]

—X:20

2 □ Stoicism and Virtue

1 The concept of love is central to Stoic philosophy. Love begins with love of self—or the love of our own rationality (the divine in us). Because this internal rational element is part of a larger rationality that encompasses all humanity, it is only natural that self-love should extend to all other beings (including our so-called enemies), both individually and collectively. This central tenet of Stoic philosophy is very similar to the Christian commandment to love God and neighbor (as self).

2 This unattributed and enigmatic hymn to love reflects the sweet notion of a yet to be created entity somehow loving the act of being created. The sentiment arises from the understanding that everything in nature is a composite of passive and active elements and that everything in nature has a soul. While only human beings have a rational soul, love, which acts like a binding force throughout all of nature, resides within the active element and is present to some degree in all of nature's creations.

3 To move is to act. Just actions are actions based on the contemplative exercise of reason, and never simply impressions of the senses. A modern version of this advice might read: stay cool; think carefully; act wisely.

4 If action is motion (something that is in our power), inaction is zero motion. In Stoic (and Newtonian) physics, as with Stoic ethics, inaction is no less relevant than action. Aurelius's words caution us that where justice demands action we have a duty to act by doing what nature commands, irrespective of any personal consequences. For example, we must not remain silent if someone is maligned. We must always act in circumstances like these, even if this action brings retribution. By the same token, when we witness injustice (racism, sexism, ageism, personal or sexual harassment, unwarranted discrimination in the workplace or elsewhere, environmental degradation), our only recourse is to use our intelligence to reverse the injustice.

☐ The Importance of Love and the Meaning of Justice

Adapt yourself to the things with which your lot has been cast: and the men and women among whom you have received your portion; love them, but do it truly, sincerely.[1]

—VI:39

"The earth loves the shower"; and "the solemn sky loves": and the universe loves to make whatever is about to be. I say then to the universe, that I love as you love. And is not this too said, that "this or that loves to be created"?[2]

—X:21

Do not be whirled about, but in every movement have respect to justice, and on the occasion of every impression maintain the faculty of comprehension or understanding.[3]

—IV:22

One may act unjustly not only through action, but through inaction.[4]

—IX:5

1 Stoics are free from pain because they are impervious to the effects of pain. They know the will of nature because they know that nature is perfect, and that whatever nature wills is part of nature's plan.

2 Every misfortune presents us with an opportunity for virtue. This is one key to remaining happy, by transforming misfortune into fortune in another guise. This might seem strange to anyone unfamiliar with the Stoic perspective. It is helpful to recall that for the Stoic none of the things we normally call misfortunes (death, ill health, losing a job, financial setbacks, and so on) are bad things in the ways we normally use the word *bad*. We may not want any of these things, but they do happen to everyone to some degree, good and bad people alike. Many of these misfortunes result from the inexorable operations of nature and, as such, can be regarded as good things. Misfortunes that arise from the willful (but ignorant) actions of others—victims of violence, for example—are never desired. This example is discussed in more detail in part 8, "The Practice of Stoicism." In any case, none of these things can ever harm our capacity for reason or our fundamental happiness, as long as we remain alive.

3 Aurelius enumerates some of the virtues that misfortune cannot touch—unless we respond with extreme grief, anger, or a desire for revenge. However, it is the duty of the Stoic to regulate the emotions. Emotional responses are fundamentally a matter of attitude (opinion), and it is always within our power to exercise control over our emotions. As a consequence, the Stoic believes that it is possible to maintain equilibrium through the power of reason—even during the most severe of human experiences.

4 Where no other option is open to us, to bear a misfortune "nobly" is itself a virtue. In this case, virtue *is* its own reward.

☐ Misfortune and Opportunity

Unhappy am I because this has happened to me. Not so, but happy am I, though this has happened to me, because I continue free from pain, neither crushed by the present nor fearing the future. For such a thing as this might have happened to every person; but every other person would not have continued free from pain on such an occasion.[1] Why then is that rather a misfortune than this a good fortune? And do you in all cases call that a person's misfortune, which is not a deviation from the nature of a human being?[2] And does a thing seem to you to be a deviation from human nature, when it is not contrary to the will of a human's nature? Well, you know the will of nature. Will then this which has happened prevent you from being just, magnanimous, temperate, prudent, and secure against inconsiderate opinions and falsehood; will it prevent you from having modesty, freedom, and everything else, by the presence of which your human nature obtains all that is its own?[3] Remember too on every occasion which leads you to exasperation to apply this principle: not that this is a misfortune, but that to bear it nobly is good fortune.[4]

—IV:49

1 This meditation offers us a concise, if somewhat cryptic, summary of Stoic morality. We first adorn ourselves with simplicity and modesty—with simplicity to remove distraction and temptation, with modesty so that we may not be blinded or absorbed in self-importance. Our response to things that lie between virtue (living according to nature) and vice (living contrary to nature) must be one of indifference. These include all of the pleasures of the world, its pains, and the trappings of wealth, fame, power, and reputation. We love humanity truly because we understand that each of us derives our faculty of reason from a common genesis—the perfect intelligence of the universe. We follow nature because in our simplicity and modesty we have witnessed nature's perfection and are drawn to this irresistibly by love. The poetry Aurelius refers to with his "Law rules all" is a reference to the *Olympian Odes* by the Greek poet Pindar (c. 518–438 BCE). Aurelius reads this line to mean a reference to the law of nature. When we study nature and understand this law, we will fully understand where our duties lie. This will be "enough."

2 This is an interesting formula. The presumption that we should act as if we are always living in our final hours certainly focuses the mind. This is a strategy that can aid us in tempering our emotional responses to indifferent experiences (becoming violently excited) and awaken our torpid (slack and lazy) minds. Aurelius returns to this theme frequently in reminding us of the brevity of life and how little time we really have to secure the tranquility that will come to us when we understand life's meaning—if we will only use our powers.

☐ Morality and the Role of Virtue

Adorn yourself with simplicity and modesty and with
indifference towards the things which lie between virtue and
vice. Love humanity. Follow nature. The poet says that Law
rules all. And it is enough to remember that Law rules all.[1]

—VII:31

The perfection of moral character consists in this, in
passing every day as the last, and in being neither violently
excited nor torpid nor playing the hypocrite.[2]

—VII:69

3 | This is a reference to Julius Caesar, who was assassinated two centuries earlier. The dye refers to Caesar's blind ambition and how this colored (dyed) his actions.

4 | The virtuous qualities Aurelius highlights throughout his *Meditations* fall into one of the four principle Stoic virtues: wisdom, justice, courage, and temperance. Piety (a respect for the natural order of things), for example, falls under justice. Many of the other qualities referred to (such as sweetness, serenity) are really emotional states. These states are not virtues as such, but emotional attitudes that encourage virtue or discourage vice.

5 | This is reference to Aurelius's adoptive father and his predecessor, Emperor Antoninus Pius, who ruled from 138 to 161. Aurelius and Pius together are referred to as the Antonines (see also the Introduction).

6 | Calumnies are false and malicious statements designed to undermine someone's reputation. As a corruption of truth, calumny is a vicious assault against reason in the Stoic view.

7 | Sophists were professional teachers in ancient Greece. In later periods, the term was applied to those who claimed to teach reasoning skill, but in fact preferred rhetorical tricks over good argument. The practice is designed to make a weak argument appear strong. Stoics saw this practice as an egregious corruption of the faculty of reason itself. Sophism survives today in some of the tactics of modern propaganda, advertising, and tabloid journalism. In the political and business arenas, the craft is sometimes called spin; a contemporary sophist is occasionally disparagingly referred to as a spin doctor.

8 | The ancient Stoics were not shy about bodily functions, but they believed the pleasures associated with those necessary acts should be confined to appropriate occasions.

Take care that you are not made into a Caesar, that you are not dyed with this dye;[3] for such things happen. Keep yourself then simple, good, pure, serious, free from affectation, a friend of justice, one who respects nature, kind, affectionate, strenuous in all proper acts. Strive to continue to be such as philosophy wishes to make you. Respect nature, and help humanity.[4] Short is life. There is only one fruit of this earthly life, a pious disposition and social acts. Do everything as a disciple of Antoninus.[5] Remember his constancy in every act which was conformable to reason, and his evenness in all things, and his piety, and the serenity of his countenance, and his sweetness, and his disregard of empty fame, and his efforts to understand things; and how he would never let anything pass without having first most carefully examined it and clearly understood it; and how he bore with those who blamed him unjustly without blaming them in return; how he did nothing in a hurry; and how he listened not to calumnies,[6] and how exact an examiner of manners and actions he was; and not given to reproach people, nor timid, nor suspicious, nor a sophist;[7] and with how little he was satisfied, such as lodging, bed, dress, food, servants; and how laborious and patient; and how he was able on account of his sparing diet to hold out to the evening, not even requiring to relieve himself by any evacuations except at the usual hour;[8] and his firmness and uniformity in his friendships; and how he tolerated freedom of speech in

(*continued on page 47*)

9 Aurelius obviously respects the wisdom of his predecessor and adoptive father, Antoninus. He also accepted policies that tolerated deviant opinions and encouraged free speech, even when those opinions were unwise. We can infer from this that Aurelius opposed censorship, a position argued convincingly in modern times by John Stuart Mill.

10 From the Stoic perspective, conscience is the power to discriminate between what is according to nature and what is contrary to nature.

11 The human constitution is the mixed composite of our material body and soul—the soul being the seat of reason.

12 Animals also have souls, but only the human animal is endowed with reason. The Stoic attributed the affinities that animals have for others of the same kind (bees in a swarm) as a manifestation of a kind of love. These attractions were attributed to a property of the active principle of nature and something humans and animals share to a degree.

13 The four virtues are perfect ideals. Acting in concert with those ideals is precisely what nature requires. These actions are used as the standards for what is right and good in moral behavior. There is no way, therefore, that any actions contrary to these perfect ideals can be considered right or good. The love of pleasure opposes the virtue of temperance because love is an attraction for things that are truly good. Aurelius does not say that pleasure itself is a vice, but pleasure is certainly not a good, and therefore can never be a virtue.

14 Aurelius likes to select examples from the boundaries of human experience. If Stoic philosophy holds up on the margins, it will certainly survive the regular exigencies of living. The fountain simile is apt. The Stoic stance promises happiness and freedom. All hardship, no matter how severe, presents an opportunity for virtue and the fulfillment of our duty to life.

those who opposed his opinions;[9] and the pleasure that he had when anyone showed him anything better; and how religious he was without superstition. Imitate all this that you may have as good a conscience, when your last hour comes, as he had.[10]

—VI:30

In the constitution[11] of the rational animal[12] I see no virtue which is opposed to justice; but I see a virtue which is opposed to love of pleasure, and that is temperance.[13]

—VIII:39

Suppose that men kill you, cut you in pieces, curse you. What then can these things do to prevent your mind from remaining pure, wise, sober, just? For instance, if a man should stand by a limpid pure spring, and curse it, the spring never ceases sending up potable water; and if he should cast clay into it or filth, it will speedily disperse them and wash them out, and will not be at all polluted. How then shall you possess a perpetual fountain and not a mere well? By forming yourself hourly to freedom surrounded with contentment, simplicity, and modesty.[14]

—VIII:51

✦ The practice of pointing to saintly role models for spiritual inspiration predates Christian tradition. Aurelius drew from the qualities of many of his relatives and political friends as a way of offering illustrations of ideal practical Stoical conduct and how their behavior influenced his own. The Stoic has a duty to live virtuously and to teach others through example. These selections serve both purposes.

1 Maximus never spoke reflexively. He considered and ordered his thoughts and spoke truly.

2 Certainly a degree of hyperbole must be at play here in the description of Maximus—few people, ancient or modern, exhibit the degree of sageness seen in many of Aurelius's acquaintances. Nonetheless, the practice of celebratory rhetoric was common in the ancient world and survives today as a style used in the writing of obituaries. Whether it is a fully accurate description or not, it is difficult to deny that the Maximus described here is a thoroughly agreeable man with qualities to which we can all aspire.

3 Aurelius's word "improved" is meant to differentiate between someone, like Maximus, who does the right thing for the right reason versus someone who may display refinement because he is simply applying the rules of etiquette.

4 This is a reminder that intelligent wit plays a role in our relationships. It challenges the contemporary perception of the Stoic as dour and humorless.

☐ Virtuous Role Models

From Maximus I learned self-government, and not to be led aside by anything; and cheerfulness in all circumstances, as well as in illness; and a just mixture in the moral character of sweetness and dignity and to do what was set before me without complaining. I observed that everybody believed that he thought as he spoke,[1] and that in all that he did he never had any bad intention; and he never showed amazement and surprise, and was never in a hurry, and never put off doing a thing, nor was perplexed nor dejected, nor did he ever laugh to disguise his aggravation, nor, on the other hand, was he ever passionate or suspicious. He was accustomed to do acts of beneficence, and was ready to forgive, and was free from all falsehood;[2] and he presented the appearance of a man who could not be diverted from right rather than of a man who had been improved.[3] I observed, too, that no man could ever think that he was despised by Maximus, or ever venture to think himself a better man. He had also the art of being humorous in an agreeable way.[4]

—I:15

5 It is during the extremes of suffering that the mettle of the Stoic is fully tested. Aurelius refers to the loss of children in several places in the *Meditations*. Aurelius would not deny the extremity of feeling in this situation. Nor would he deny the profound love of a parent for a child or ask us to deny this loss. Before Christianity, Stoicism was unique in its idea of the universality of love as expressed toward all members of the human family, including our enemies. But the key feature of Stoic practice reinforced here is the capacity to notice strong feelings without giving assent.

✦ This aspect of Stoicism has a parallel in Buddhism, where the practitioner strives to sever attachments to certain feelings to avoid either cravings (in the case of pleasurable feelings) or aversions (around painful feelings). In outward appearance, these practices may seem cold and heartless. Nothing is farther from the truth. From the Stoic perspective, the affects, or emotional states, that arise from heartfelt responses to the extremes of pain (or pleasure) enslave reason and limit the will. In some situations, these feelings can lead to compulsive addictions (to pleasures) or paralyzing fears (of pain and suffering). In both cases, our capacity to reason well or to exercise virtue becomes severely limited.

6 By simplicity, Aurelius is not advocating asceticism or poverty. The direction to simplicity is designed to minimize complications arising from excess. Of the particular Roman virtues *gravitas* (depth of personality), *dignitas* (prestige and influence), and *pietas* (piety and duty), the last merits special attention. In Roman society, *pietas* was expressed through a series of devotional duties and rituals following extended family lines between parent and child, between husband and wife, and between the living and the dead. The concept extended upward to include relationships between the citizen and the state. Children were expected to honor their parents, and parents to love their children. Citizens were expected to honor the state. These duties were performed within the context of an extended and sacred family unit.

From Apollonius I learned freedom of will and undeviating steadiness of purpose; and to look to nothing else, not even for a moment, except to reason; and to be always the same, in sharp pains, on the occasion of the loss of a child, and in long illness.[5]

—I:8

From my mother, [I learned] piety and beneficence, and abstinence, not only from evil deeds, but even from evil thoughts; and further, simplicity in my way of living, far removed from the habits of the rich.[6]

—I:3

7 Friendship is important in the world of the Stoic; we must look carefully after our friends, because friends are regarded as extensions of the shared intelligence of the universe—or literally as other selves. Tolerance is also important. Given the value attached to Sextus's virtues, it is difficult to imagine a Stoic acting out because of road rage or displaying indignation at a profound stupidity.

8 As mentioned in the Introduction, Aurelius was three years old when his father, Marcus Annius Verus, died in 124 CE, after which Marcus was raised by his paternal grandfather, also named Marcus Annius Verus. The reputation of both men had a large influence on the young Aurelius. These were qualities Aurelius valued and imitated in his own leadership style: mildness, decisiveness, modesty, hard work, excellent listening skills, justice, experience, affable and effective communications, mercy, gentleness, and non-affectation. The last of these implies that the virtues these men displayed were genuine and never a matter of show. Each of us in our own spheres of influence as well as modern leaders of business and politics might want to take note of this list—although the last quality might present a problem for some.

From Sextus, [I learned] a benevolent disposition, and the example of a family governed in a wise manner, and the idea of living conformably to nature; and gravity without affectation, and to look carefully after the interests of friends, and to tolerate ignorant persons, and those who form opinions without consideration.[7]

—I:9

In my father I observed mildness of temper, and unchangeable resolution in the things which he had determined after due deliberation; and no excessive pride in those things which people call honors; and a love of labor and perseverance; and a readiness to listen to those who had anything to propose for the state; and undeviating firmness in giving to every person according to what they deserve; and a knowledge derived from experience of the occasions for vigorous action and for remission.... He was also easy in conversation, and he made himself agreeable without any offensive affectation.... There was in him nothing harsh, nor implacable, nor violent.[8]

—I:16

3 □ Stoicism and Vice

1 If it is right, do it; if it is true, teach it. Aurelius casts his meditation in the negative because those who understand the true nature of what is right are likely to do the right thing. Aurelius probably feels no need to preach to the converted.

2 These are four examples of vices (or evils) we bring onto ourselves by the corruption of reason: hate (from despising), hypocrisy (from flattering), pretension (from raising ourselves above one another), and pandering (from crouching before one another).

3 This is how the Stoic explains evil. Anything we do that limits our ability to use our reason is evil. Reason comes to us from nature and is at the heart of natural law. Its corruption is contrary to nature. When we lose reason, we isolate ourselves from other human beings because reason is the only thing that all humans share. Reason is the source of our freedom and power to act as nature ordains. Without reason, we are enslaved by the whims of others and the sensations of the body and are unable to experience happiness. In this state, our actions are restricted to the attractions of our animal nature: the pursuit of pleasure or power, and the avoidance of pain. But none of these things is ever within our power. All pleasures are illusory and temporary, and they depend to some degree on the cooperation of others, or luck.

+ This explanation of evil and how it works contrasts with alternative views that portray evil as an infection—caused either by some external agency (like Satan) or an idea (like terrorism)—which, if unchecked, might spread, like an epidemic sweeping up innocent victims. The Stoic concept of evil is located exclusively inside the mind of the actor, "whoever does wrong does wrong against himself." A Stoic will not deny that terrible misfortunes (murder, war, genocide) are consequences of evil. But the Stoic maintains that as horrific as these consequences are, there is no reason that any misfortune will, in and of itself, corrupt the ruling capacity of a victim, because reason is always immune from harm. It is only in reason that our authentic humanity resides.

(continued on page 58)

☐ The Nature of Evil and Insignificance of Misfortune

If it is not right, do not do it: if it is not true, do not say it.[1]

—XII:17

People despise one another and flatter one another and wish to raise themselves above one another, and crouch before one another.[2]

—XI:14

Whoever does wrong does wrong against himself. He who acts unjustly acts unjustly to himself, because he makes himself bad.[3]

—IX:4

The difference between the two explanations of evil results in different attitudes about how we should respond. Both versions trigger a strong and dutiful response. But the urgency of some contemporary responses to evil—such as the need to declare a war on evil (or a war on terror)—is supplanted in the Stoic with a compassion for the perpetrators of evil, and a concomitant duty to remove the ignorance that gives rise to evil.

4 This passage instructs us how to maintain equilibrium in our emotional lives. While emotions serve a useful purpose, the Stoic always strives to keep perspective around these feelings. Stoics will enjoy ice cream and feel discomfort on a hot day. But Stoics will avoid labeling the feelings associated with those things as good or bad. In so doing, they avoid falling into the hedonistic belief that life revolves around the pursuit of pleasure or the avoidance of discomfort. The true good and bad things in life devolve from living within the demands of nature—and that means living a life of virtue and directing our actions toward the benefit of others. Stoics believe that in labeling the emotional feelings associated with pleasure or pain as good or bad, we risk developing false values—a habit that in the longer run can lead to evil outcomes. How do we learn to control our feelings when dealing with an emotional response? The litmus test is whether the emotional impression provokes an irrational affect, or emotional state. For a Stoic, the appropriate response to a negative situation should be concern or caution. If a situation provokes extreme anxiety, worry, envy, or fear, we need to reevaluate this emotional response. A rational reassessment will invariably demonstrate that any one of these overreactions comes from irrationally assigning a good or bad value to the impression that caused the feeling. In simple terms, if an emotional situation makes us unhappy, we need to reevaluate. As Stoics, we should never feel unhappy. This does not mean we should feel nothing, but what we feel should never impede our capacity to act rationally.

Never value anything as profitable to yourself which shall
compel you to break your promise, to lose your self-
respect, to hate any person, to suspect, to curse, to act the
hypocrite, to desire anything which needs walls and
curtains: for the person who has preferred to everything
intelligence and spirit and the worship of its excellence,
acts no tragic part, does not groan, will not need either
solitude or much company; and, what is chief of all, will
live without either pursuing or flying from death.[4]

—III:7

5   These five Stoic intellectual guidelines, or so-called commandments, come not from God but from reason. Each of these can be viewed as a transgression (sin) against reason. We become alienated from reason when we act in these ways. For Aurelius, irritability, antisocial behavior, excess passion, dishonesty, and thoughtlessness are tears in the fabric of nature, because each of these activities breaches our capacity for reason—the source of the only powers that are truly ours and the basis of what make us human.

✦   Christians have an alternative position on alienation. They consider humanity as initially alienated from God through original sin. Redemption removes original sin through Christ, who is theologically identified as the "word" or *Logos* made flesh. Both Christians and Stoics direct their love toward the *Logos*, and both regard the *Logos* as divine. The difference, of course, is that Stoics regard *Logos* as in us from our beginnings, an integral part of our human nature, and a material substance that permeates the whole universe. Christians, on the other hand, regard *Logos* as a spirit person in a triune God, who enters human nature through an act of faith and guides human action as the living Christ. Eastern philosophical and religious traditions also retain concepts with certain similarities to the *Logos* of Stoicism and Christianity. These include the *Tao*, or Way of Nature, as expressed in Chinese traditions; the Vedic concept of *rta*, the order or course of things; the Buddhist dharma, the underlying order of nature; and the Hindu *Aum*, the beginning and end of all things.

The soul does violence to itself, first of all, when it becomes an abscess and a tumor on the universe, so far as it can. For to be annoyed at anything which happens is a separation of ourselves from nature, in some part of which the natures of all other things are contained. In the next place, the soul does violence to itself when it turns away from any person, or even moves towards another with the intention of injuring, such as are the souls of those who are angry. In the third place, the soul does violence to itself when it is overpowered by pleasure or by pain. Fourthly, when it plays a part, and does or says anything insincerely and untruly. Fifthly, when it allows any act of its own and any movement to be without an aim, and does anything thoughtlessly and without considering what it is, it being right that even the smallest things be done with reference to an end; and the end of rational animals is to follow the reason and the law of the most ancient city and polity.[5]

—II:16

6 Impiety or profanity is any abuse of the natural order. Mocking these duties, or violating them, is profane and unjust because it is contrary to the natural order of things. Each of the transgressions discussed in the passage is profane because it goes against one of the five Stoic commandments: (1) You shall not be annoyed. (2) You shall not withdraw from others. (3) Pleasure or pain shall not overpower you. (4) You shall not be dishonest. (5) You shall not act without thinking.

7 Lying is a violation of the fourth Stoic commandment, the abuse of truth.

8 To lie unintentionally is a form of inaction, and a violation of the fifth Stoic commandment, to act without thinking.

9 To be overpowered by pleasure or pain is a violation of the third Stoic commandment because this robs us of our real powers—the use of our reason. This idea is extraordinarily important in the life of a Stoic. Those who identify pleasure and pain as the most important values in life develop distorted thinking, irrational fears, false values, and corrupted reason. The corruption of reason leads to spiritual malaise and doubt. For example, a Stoic would never raise the following objection: "If there is Providence in the universe, why do bad things happen to good people?" The Stoic would reason that what we label bad comes from giving assent to impressions around which we ought to remain indifferent. In the absence of such assent, the Stoic might answer: "Bad things never happen to good people. Good people are immune from evil." The things most of us call bad are not so to the Stoic—they are misfortunes.

The person who acts unjustly acts profanely [impiously]. For since the universal nature has made rational animals for the sake of one another to help one another according to what is deserved by them, but in no way to injure one another, the person who transgresses her will, is clearly guilty of profanity towards the highest principle.[6] And the person who lies is also guilty of profanity; for the universal nature is the nature of things that are; and things that are have a relation to all things that come into existence. And further, this universal nature is named truth, and is the prime cause of all things that are true. The person who lies intentionally is guilty of profanity inasmuch as this act of deceit is unjust.[7] The person who lies unintentionally is also guilty of profanity because this act contradicts the nature and order of the world—for anyone who fights against this order is moving in contradiction to truth. For this person had received powers from nature but through the neglect of these powers is not able now to distinguish falsehood from truth.[8] And indeed the person who pursues pleasure as good, and avoids pain as evil, is guilty also of profanity. Such a person must of necessity often find fault with the universal nature by alleging that the universal nature assigns things to the bad and the good contrary to what is deserved by them. Such a person will find fault also because frequently the bad enjoy pleasure and possess the things which procure pleasure, but the good have pain for their share in the things which cause pain. And further, the person who fears pain will sometimes also be afraid of some of the things which will happen in the world, and even this is profanity. And the person who pursues pleasure will not abstain from injustice, and this is plainly profane.[9]

—IX: 1

1 Aurelius is asking us to consider the source whenever we seek approval (or praise) from others. This approval may be based on a false opinion (such as ignorance about virtue) or a false appetite (the belief that pleasure is a good). In either case, those who offer approval do so for the wrong reasons. Aurelius also offers this argument to those who seek fame.

2 This passage is a beautiful example of traditional formal logic applied to those who seek (or avoid) praise. Logic is one of the three pillars of Stoic philosophy: physics, logic, and ethics. Physics teaches that reason is at the center of existence. Logic teaches how to use reason. Ethics teaches how to live the good life through reason. What, if any, value can there be in seeking the praise of those who have no idea of life's purpose? The first step in this logical sequence is the application of physics to the study of the world. Through physics you see the world's design, structure, and composition and begin to understand where you are.

3 The application of physics (in this case, Stoic physics) to the world reveals a universe comprised of passive and active principles with a design and purpose. We see that our human nature is a mixture of these same principles, so we, too, must have a design and a purpose conforming to the larger world.

4 If we do not know what the world is, we cannot possibly understand who we are. This leaves us lost and alone, lacking direction and purpose. The only purpose people like these can see for life comes from the sensations of the body. Such people seek pleasure or avoid pain, and they praise (or blame) others when they assist (or aggravate) these things.

5 This is the context we use in assessing the value we attach to praise or blame. If praise or blame comes from those who see life's purpose in terms of pleasure or pain, what reason do we have for valuing their opinions?

☐ Never Seek Praise and Never Blame Others

Constantly observe who those are whose approval you wish to have, and what ruling principles they possess. For then you will neither blame those who offend involuntarily, nor will you want their approval, if you look to the sources of their opinions and appetites.[1]

—VII:62

If you do not know what the world is, you know not where you are.[2] If you do not know for what purpose the world exists, you know not who you are, or what the world is.[3] If you fail in any one of these things you know not for what purpose you exist.[4] What then do you think of those who avoid or seek the praise of those who applaud, of those who know not either where they are or who they are?[5]

—VIII:52

1 The passage asks us to wipe out imagination, desire, and appetite. This seems like a strong command. Aurelius is aware that many people tend to respond emotionally—in other words, they act first and think later. The meditation is not about the elimination of pleasure or appetite (desire for future pleasure). It is designed to help us think about the proper relationship between reason (rational behavior) and the emotions (irrational behavior). The emotions serve an essential role in life, but our actions always need to be mediated by reason.

2 Our capacity to form an evil opinion is part of our free will. But the evil opinion itself is our own. This is because an evil opinion is by definition against reason. Reason in itself is completely good and cannot suffer or cause harm. Evil is also irrational, while reason is rational. An evil opinion can be shared by more than one person, but the locus of this sharing is outside of reason—it "does not subsist in the ruling principle of another."

3 There is nothing evil about the body. This is an interesting feature of Stoicism. The material composition of the body comes from the passive principle of nature. The body simply *is*. We may use the body in the service of virtue or vice, but there is nothing about the body itself or of any of its functions that we can ever call good or bad.

4 The human will is free and independent. By free, Aurelius means we have the power to form opinions and act either according to nature (with virtue) or contrary to nature (with vice). The will is independent in that no evil act by another can harm our ruling principle.

5 As discussed before, bad things cannot happen to good people. Misfortunes can happen to anyone, but misfortune never harms our ruling principles. Aurelius revisits the idea again here from the point of view of reason. Bodily injury, disease, or accidents (misfortunes) happen to good and bad people equally. But these things do not depend on virtue or vice.

☐ Stoic Psychology, Alienation, and Free Will

Wipe out imagination; check desire; extinguish appetite; keep the ruling faculty in its own power.[1]

—IX:7

What is evil to you does not subsist in the ruling principle of another;[2] nor yet in any turning and mutation of your corporeal covering.[3] Where is it then? It is in that part of you which subsists in the power of forming opinions about evils. Let this power then not form such opinions, and all is well.[4] And if that which is nearest to it, the poor body, is burnt, filled with matter and rottenness, nevertheless let the part which forms opinions about these things be quiet, that is, let it judge that nothing is either bad or good which can happen equally to the bad person and the good. For that which happens equally to who lives contrary to nature and to who lives according to nature, is neither according to nature nor contrary to nature.[5]

—IV:39

6 Alienation from our true nature is an inevitable consequence of any one or all of several psychosocial disturbances. The Aurelius litany has a disturbingly modern ring: self-centeredness, codependence, ignorance and irrationality, intellectual apathy, terrorism and other antisocial and criminal behaviors. It requires little imagination to see where Aurelius is headed with this. The self-absorbed "runaway" has no interest in anything other than personal goals. He will have a social life, but those connections are directed toward personal advancement or getting ahead.

7 The "blind" man is closed to all reason. For him, life is a series of sensations: the satisfactions of pleasure and the avoidance of discomfort.

8 The "poor" man who has need of another is codependent on others for all useful things. He is always a follower. He depends on others to think for him, having surrendered his intellectual sovereignty to a partner, an employer, a cult, or in some cases even a fanatical political movement.

9 The "abscess on the universe" is the man who is displeased and angry with everything. He is willing to do anything contrary to nature to mollify his bitterness, from criminal activity and political terrorism to self-destructive behavior.

10 The psychological and sociological damage from these alienations is immeasurable. But for Aurelius the damage is correctable—not through behavioral modification, psychotropic drugs, psychotherapy, or mass incarceration—but through philosophy. Teach and model respect and love of the unity and beneficence of nature and live according to its demands.

If you are a stranger to the universe and do not know what
is in it, you are also a stranger who does not know what is
going on in it. You are a runaway, who flies from social
reason;[6] you are blind, who shuts the eyes of the
understanding;[7] you are poor, who has need of another, and
has not from yourself all things which are useful for life.[8]
You are an abscess on the universe who withdraws and
separates yourself from the reason of our common nature
through being displeased with the things which happen, for
the same nature produces this, and has produced you too:
you are a piece rent asunder from the state[9] who tears your
own soul from that of reasonable animals, which is one.[10]

—IV:29

1 This is how Stoics manage anger. Agitation can serve a useful purpose and is part of our animal nature. But uncontrolled anger clouds our capacity to react rationally. Anger is triggered when we fear harm—real or imagined. This is, of course, an illusory fear because reason is immune from harm. Anger will dissipate when we replace fears with concern, or caution. This allows us to restore the mental clarity needed to respond with reason. Aurelius later offers a ten-step program in anger management (see part 8, "The Practice of Stoicism").

2 This is an interesting example of compassion and empathy toward those whose actions are clearly wrong. While it may be our duty to correct error, we have no less a duty to do so in a sensitive and forgiving way. If someone believes in what he or she is doing or saying, we need to try to understand that person's motives and intentions. Berating or coldly correcting a wrongdoer is not only counterproductive, but it is also vindictive and will likely be received as a put-down. Pointing out error with sensitivity and understanding requires skill and psychology. If our intention is really designed to change an opinion, then we need to do so with tact and respect.

3 The ruling faculty is reason. It is constituted so that we may act socially and act outwardly with virtue and in the interests of others. We are discontented with this when we desire to act inwardly with self-interest.

4 Discontent is a generalized malaise. This condition results when our opinions about the things we think are good for us are directed toward personal self-interest. Aurelius refers to those who may play by the rules of reason but do so begrudgingly because the real objects of value in their lives lie elsewhere (in pleasures, or wealth, or fame). His abrupt, cursory "enough of this" contrasts with the boundlessness of the "infinite troubles" that discontent will bring: troubles be gone!

☐ The Problem with Anger and Discontent

When you have been compelled by circumstances to become agitated, quickly return to yourself and do not continue out of tune longer than the compulsion lasts; for you will have more mastery over the harmony by continually returning to reason.[1]

—VI:11

How cruel it is not to allow people to strive after the things which appear to them to be suitable to their nature and profitable! And yet in a manner you do not allow them to do this, when you are agitated because they do wrong. For they are certainly moved towards things because they suppose them to be suitable to their nature and profitable to them; but it is not so. Teach them then, and show them without being angry.[2]

—VI:27

You have endured infinite troubles through not being contented with your ruling faculty, when it does the things which it is constituted by nature to do.[3] But enough of this.[4]

—IX:26

1 The superior human faculty is the mind. Characterizing undesired behaviors as aberrations is consistent with the idea that actions contrary to nature emerge more from ignorance than from wickedness. Aurelius does not deny the possibility that human beings can willfully make evil choices. But because we cannot easily discern human motives, it is better to presume mitigating reasons for aberrant behaviors. This approach allows Aurelius to explore a range of psychological abnormalities that can occur as a consequence of ignorance.

2 In Stoic psychology, aberrations of thought present themselves as behavioral patterns arising from compulsive noncompliance with Stoic commandments and principles. The aberrations or thought patterns we are in danger of acquiring as a consequence fall into four categories: (1) unnecessary or fanciful, (2) antisocial, (3) delusional, and (4) obsessional. In essence, these thought patterns arise from faulty value assignments, such as valuing the wrong things (placing the personal before the social, or valuing the pleasures of the body over the mind), fearing the wrong dangers (fearing pain over evil), or assenting to the wrong impressions (yielding to the desires of the body over the mind). The treatment of these aberrations in each case involves watchful attention. A Stoic must be aware that these thoughts keep us from acting according to nature. They prevent us from using our reason effectively, and they make us unhappy. We can avoid or extinguish the patterns by refusing to yield to or give assent to each thought as it arises and by following a specific procedure, as noted in the next meditation.

☐ Stoicism and Mental Health

There are four principal aberrations of the superior faculty[1]
against which you should be constantly on your guard, and
when you have detected them, you should wipe them out
and say on each occasion thus: (1) this thought is not
necessary; (2) this tends to destroy social union; (3) this
which you are going to say comes not from the real
thoughts, for you should consider it among the most absurd
of things not to speak from your real thoughts; (4) the last
is when you reproach yourself for anything, for this is an
evidence of the more perfect part within you being
overpowered and yielding to the less honorable and to the
perishable part, the body, and to its gross pleasures.[2]

—XI:19

3 | This meditative exercise in self-analysis is done with perfect honesty. The approach is honest in its sensual purity and personal sincerity. Stoicism was unique in antiquity for its liberality. It was intolerant of slavery, gender oppression, racial discrimination, ageism, elitism, classicism, and self-aggrandizement. Because every rational animal is our kin, all human beings were considered equal, regardless of sex, talents, age, race, or station. Every human being is capable of virtue and potentially worthy of being included as "among the number of the best people." Acting rightly, or being virtuous, was not graded. All virtuous acts were equal, regardless of rank or impact.

We ought then to check in the series of our thoughts everything that is without a purpose and useless, but most of all the over-curious feeling and the malignant. Think only those thoughts that, should you ask yourself: *What have I now in my thoughts?* With perfect openness you might, immediately answer: *this or that;* so that from your words it should be plain that everything in you is simple and benevolent, and such as befits a social animal, and one that cares not for thoughts about pleasure or sensual enjoyments at all, nor has any rivalry or envy or suspicion, or anything else for which you would blush if you should say that you had it in your mind. For if you are such and no longer delay being among the number of the best people, you are like a priest and minister of nature, using too the ruling intelligence which is planted inside you, which makes you uncontaminated by pleasure, unharmed by any pain, untouched by any insult, feeling no wrong, a fighter in the noblest fight, one who cannot be overpowered by any passion, dyed deep with justice, accepting with all your soul everything which happens and is assigned to you as your portion.... Remember also that every rational animal is your kin, and that to care for all human beings is according to your human nature; and you should hold on to the opinion not of all, but of those only who confessedly live according to nature. But as to those who live not so, always bear in mind what kind of men and women they are both at home and from home, both by night and by day, and what they are, and with what men and women they live an impure life. Accordingly, you do not value at all the praise which comes from such men and women, since they are not even satisfied with themselves.[3]

—III:4

4   This intense passage speaks to those who are determined to abide by vice—in other words, to live contrary to nature by abandoning virtue altogether. Aurelius refers to this complete dereliction of human duty as the "destruction or corruption of the understanding." In Stoic terms, this is vice in the raw—comparable perhaps to the controversial Christian idea of the "unforgivable sin," which entails the rejection of the spirit of God. What does Aurelius recommend here when he says that "to breathe out one's life when you have had enough of these things is the next best voyage"? It could well mean that while it is best to live a life free of these things, if that's not possible, then next best is to live long enough so that you get your fill of such things and hence finally see their futility before you die. A controversial interpretation is that taking one's own life would be the only noble way to deal with this. This possibility was not original to the Stoics. In his *Laws*, Plato argued that while suicide was a disgraceful act, there were a few exceptions. One was when the mind was morally and irreparably corrupt. The Roman Stoic Seneca (3 BCE–65 CE), who eventually took his own life, claimed that a wise person "lives as long as he ought, not as long as he can." Whatever the case, Aurelius refers to the subject of suicide far less often than his Stoic predecessors did. The tone of the *Meditations* is tender, compassionate, and forgiving.

On the other hand, as we will see in part 4, "Stoicism and the Body," death is no huge occurrence in the Stoic universe. Death is really an incidental event with no bearing on the true meaning of life. While no Stoic would prefer death under normal circumstances, there might well be situations where death should not be rejected if continuing to live means living contrary to nature.

It would be your happiest lot to depart from life without having had any taste of lying and hypocrisy and luxury and pride. However to breathe out one's life when you have had enough of these things is the next best voyage, as the saying is. Have you determined to abide with vice, and has not experience yet induced you to fly from this pestilence? For the destruction of the understanding is a pestilence, much more indeed than any such corruption and change of this atmosphere which surrounds us. For this corruption is a pestilence of animals so far as they are animals; but the other is a pestilence of men and women so far as they are men and women.[4]

—IX:2

1 Aurelius is not being cynical about self-love. Stoic philosophy actually begins with love of self. As humans mature, the self that one loves shifts from body to mind. This in turn matures into a love of others, and finally to the universe as a whole. Aurelius's comment on the "opinion of others" refers to the false opinion of those who live contrary to nature. As Aurelius describes in a previous meditation, we are not discouraged from considering the opinions of those who live according to nature. The development of opinion is a social and cooperative program, as will be discussed more fully in part 6, "The Method of Stoicism."

2 Phocion (c. 402–c. 318 BCE) was an Athenian statesman with a reputation for integrity.

3 The interior parts refer to the life of the mind.

4 The example is offered here to demonstrate mildness and benevolence in the face of hatred and contempt. It is sufficient simply to be undeserving of contempt. The nonviolent sentiment is similar in tone to Jesus's refutation of revenge in Matthew 5:38–39: "You have heard that it was said, 'An eye for an eye and a tooth for a tooth.' But I say to you, do not resist an evildoer. But if anyone strikes you on the right cheek, turn the other also."

5 When our actions are synchronous with the will of nature, we are impervious to harm and are moving inexorably along the path of destiny.

☐ Ignoring What Others Think

I have often wondered how it is that every man has more love of himself than all the rest of the world, but yet sets less value on his own opinion of himself than on the opinion of others.[1]

—XII:4

Suppose anyone shall despise me. Let that one look to that herself. But I will look to this, that I be not discovered doing or saying anything deserving of contempt. Shall anyone hate me? Let that one look to it. But I will be mild and benevolent towards everyone, and ready to show even the mistake that one makes, not reproachfully, nor yet as making a display of my endurance, but nobly and honestly, like the great Phocion[2]—unless indeed he only assumed it. For the interior parts[3] ought to be such, and one ought to be seen by nature neither dissatisfied with anything nor complaining.[4] For what evil is it to you, if you are now doing what is agreeable to your own nature, and are satisfied with that which at this moment is suitable to the nature of the universe, since you are a human being placed at your post in order that what is for the common advantage may be done in some way?[5]

—XI:13

6 The Stoic puts the mind before the body, and social duty before personal duty. The leading principles of those who live contrary to nature would reverse these.

7 This is a Stoic version of the expression "The proof is in the pudding." Aurelius's comments are directed toward those who live contrary to nature and the praise they may offer. Someone who lives contrary to nature is unable to offer praise because he is unaware of the principles or criteria that the Stoic uses if offering praise.

The language Aurelius uses mocks attempts to offer praise by inviting us to imagine the souls of such people laid bare. This suggests a certain degree of absurdity in the very idea that anyone detached from nature could have any influence on anything that mattered. This does not imply that ignorant people (those who are unaware of nature's law) are incapable of causing terrible misfortune. Ignorance in a democracy, for example, can put unqualified people in offices of great power, where they may create destruction and havoc in the world. But, for the Stoic, this never causes real harm, because human beings can never be prevented from using their reason.

This does not mean that Stoics would sit idly by or watch these things with disinterest. The Stoic response to misfortune is always one of concern or caution; no Stoic wants to see a world in havoc. Stoics prefer peace. In fact, this is the source of their courage. Because they do not fear pain or retribution, they are far less likely to worry about personal physical or economic security when dealing with a major political, personal, or environmental crisis.

What are the leading principles[6] of these men and women, and about what kind of things are they busy, and for what kind of reasons do they love and honor? Imagine that you see their poor souls laid bare. When they think that they do harm by their blame or good by their praise, what an idea![7]

—IX:34

8 The term "in a round" refers to a theatrical staging where the audience is seated on all sides of the stage. This setup was common in the arena configurations of ancient Greece and Rome, where plays were performed in a pit below the level of the audience.

9 The reference is to the ancient Greek playwright Aristophanes (c. 448– c. 388 BCE) and his comic satire *The Clouds,* which pokes fun at Socrates and his philosophical musings. In the play, Socrates is caricaturized as head of the "Thinkery." Socrates first appears in the play suspended high above the stage with his head "in the clouds," so as to breathe the purer air more suitable for his lofty ideas about things above and "beneath the earth."

Although the play misrepresents the real-life Socrates, it was enormously successful, and Plato was rumored to have kept a copy under his pillow. The play as satire was intended as a critique of sophism—the practice of making an inherently weak argument appear strong—a technique that people with false opinions were prone to try. Socrates himself was not a sophist, but many in the audience of his day would not know that, or be able to tell the difference. Aurelius (and Aristophanes) of course admired the real Socrates, and he assumes in this note that readers would be well aware of the distinction between Socrates and his satirized character in the play. Unfortunately, the play had a negative influence on the real Socrates and appears to have been influential in swaying the jury that convicted him of sedition in a close vote (280 in favor vs. 221 opposed) in 399 BCE.

10 Stoics have no direct concern for or power over the opinions of others, particularly the opinions of those who do not follow nature. Stoics do have power over their own opinions and would be open to the opinions of those who follow nature, as well as a duty to nurture that spirit according to the dictates of nature.

11 Unlike elitist philosophies that require years of reading or schooling, Stoicism requires only that we understand that happiness comes from virtue and by avoiding irritability, antisocial behavior, excess passion, dishonesty, and thoughtlessness (these are the five Stoic commandments).

Nothing is more wretched than someone who traverses everything in a round,[8] and pries into the things beneath the earth,[9] as the poet says, and seeks by conjecture what is in the minds of neighbors, without perceiving that it is sufficient to attend to the spirit inside, and to respect it truthfully.[10]

—II:13

You have not leisure or ability to read. But you have leisure or ability to overcome arrogance: you have leisure to be superior to pleasure and pain: you have leisure to be superior to love of fame, and not to be annoyed at stupid and ungrateful people and even to care for them.[11]

—VIII:8

1 Human intelligence is derived from the "intelligence of the universe," or the active principle of nature, also called *Logos*. It is this common origin that unifies and connects all human beings in their many social relationships. These relationships include political communities, which are built on common values. Those values include shared beliefs about moral or ethical ideas of right and wrong. But in a world where morals are a matter of convention, right or wrong will depend upon the culture or religion or educational system in that culture. There is no guarantee, therefore, that any two distinct cultures will ever share the same set of values. In other words, morality is relative. If the political culture in any place grows out of the moral traditions in that location, then the political culture in another place would differ if the moral traditions there differed. This moral relativity implies political relativity, neither of which is consistent with the Stoic concept of a universal intelligence.

✦ The moral and political variations discussed above can extend right on down to personal experience. In such a world, my moral standards might differ from yours, if my cultural, religious, educational and personal experience also differs from yours. The idea of competing moralities is completely at odds with the Stoic understanding of the world, where a single and universal moral standard as revealed by nature is the sole reference for virtue. Marcus Aurelius would see these alternate moralities as false opinions and contrary to nature. Canadian philosopher Charles Taylor (b. 1931) argues that moral relativity in the world today is responsible for what he calls the "Malaise of Modernity," and he considers this malaise a major source of the unease of the modern world.

2 Aurelius advises us here that our moral and political values must be universal because we share the same natural law—universal intelligence—from which all true values are derived. Aurelius notes also that all the world is "in a manner a state" and that every member of the human race belongs to this state. We could infer from this that Aurelius would also advocate a single world government. But nowhere does Aurelius tell us how such a government might come about.

☐ Moral Relativism

The intelligence of the universe is social.[1]

—V:30

If our intellectual part is common to all, the reason also, in respect of which we are rational beings, is common: if this is so, common also is the reason which commands us what to do, and what not to do; if this is so, there is a common law also; if this is so, we are fellow-citizens; if this is so, we are members of some political community; if this is so, the world is in a manner a state. What other common political community will anyone say that every member of the human race belongs? And from there, from this common political community, comes also our very intellectual faculty and reasoning faculty and our capacity for law.[2]

—IV:4

4 □ Stoicism and the Body

1 Aurelius has a sense of humor, yet the aphorism makes its point. The physical package is but an ephemeral, fragile, irrelevant, and temporary thing.

2 For Aurelius, *undisturbed* means not to give assent. A toothache is a toothache; a fine wine is a fine wine. The soul or reason will remain itself unchanged by toothaches or wine. This idea is remarkably similar to the teachings of Buddhism, where it is our thoughts that turn a thing (for example, pain) into suffering. The Third Noble Truth in Buddhist teaching presents a way of ending suffering by letting go of those thoughts about how we believe things ought to be.

3 The affects, or the emotional states, induced by a toothache (or wine) will naturally inform reason, and it is senseless to deny or to resist those feelings. Stoicism isn't about denial or deprivation, but about seeing things as they are and nothing more. We do this by controlling the role of imagination (mind) in amplifying the pains (or pleasures) of the body (matter) into things that are much greater than they are. This is how the Stoic controls mind over matter.

4 From a moral perspective, a toothache or a glass of wine is just what it is and nothing more. There is nothing inherently good or bad about either of the sensations associated with these. To claim otherwise would elevate a physical sensation to the rank of a virtue or a vice. To Aurelius, this is irrational.

☐ Mind over Matter

You are a little soul bearing about a corpse.[1]

—IV:41

Let the part of your soul which leads and governs be undisturbed by the movements in the flesh, whether of pleasure or of pain; and let it not unite with them, but let it circumscribe itself and limit those affects to their parts.[2] But when these affects rise up to the mind by virtue of that other sympathy that naturally exists in a body which is all one, then you must not strive to resist the sensation, for it is natural:[3] but let not the ruling part of itself add to the sensation the opinion that it is either good or bad.[4]

—V:26

1 From a Stoic perspective, stealing, murder, and tyranny are unfortunate consequences of social withdrawal, dishonesty, and thoughtlessness—three traits we are warned against by the Stoic commandments. The Stoic commandments might seem mild in comparison to the comparable prohibitions within the Judeo-Christian tradition, where it is the consequences (not the mental attitudes) that are expressly forbidden—in this case, violations of the fifth (on stealing), seventh (on murder), and tenth commandments (on coveting the property and freedom of others). In the Stoic scheme, stealing, murder, and tyranny are outcomes that flow from distorted thinking and the abandonment of reason. The focus of the meditation is to question the role of pleasure in the lives of the perpetrators of these crimes. We are meant to see the tragic irony in the extreme and unpleasant actions carried out by those who have falsely made pleasure the focus of their lives.

2 Modern science might take issue with the view that the universe exists for some purpose, or that it is following a predetermined plan. But is it relevant whether the universe is unfolding purposefully, or whether it is following a pattern consistent with the indeterminacies of modern chaos theory? What matters is that Stoicism was meant to be an evolving ethical system that attempted to pattern morality on the laws of nature—whatever they are. The ethical norms of the Stoics are no less valid today than they were in the second century, when we were looking at the cosmos through a glass darkly.

The ancient Stoics professed that what we ought to do morally was informed by the way the world was. They professed, for example, that the sun has many purposes. One of those is consistent with the evolution of and propagation of human life and reason. It is within this context that we should see the logic of Aurelius's critique that a human life founded on pleasure is purposeless. Today, we can look at the sun and planets in ways the ancients could not. We observe a system of bodies adhering to each other under the law of gravitation, a concept unknown to the ancient Stoics. But it is certain that if the Stoics did

(continued on page 92)

☐ The Stoic Attitude toward Pleasure

How many pleasures have been enjoyed by robbers,
patricides, tyrants.[1]

—VI:34

Everything exists for some end, be it a horse or a vine. Why
do you wonder? Even the sun will say, I am for some
purpose, and the rest of nature will say the same. For what
purpose then are you? to enjoy pleasure? See if common
sense allows this.[2]

—VIII:19

discover the gravitational cooperation between the earth and the sun, this new example of affinity in nature would reinforce their belief that we as human beings are also under the sway of analogous cooperative social laws. This is the way the Stoics looked at nature for guidance. To the Stoic, a human being guided by a self-serving purpose—such as pleasure—is as senseless as a rogue planet. No planet in our system has the right to quit the solar system. By analogy, no human being has a right to operate as a rogue in a world governed by social principles. Anyone who tries will be consumed by unhappiness and despair.

3 | This seems like a strange definition for repentance. Most people would define repentance as remorse for doing something wrong. But Aurelius defines repentance here as neglecting something useful. It is helpful to remember that for the Stoic the only useful things are good things, and the only truly good things are virtuous acts. So repentance in this passage really refers to the neglect of virtue.

4 | The perfect good person will never neglect useful things. He will "look after it." He will never forget his first duty: to be virtuous toward others, even when those virtuous actions seem small and insignificant.

5 | Would I repent giving up a sensual pleasure such as not having a glass of fine wine? Applying Aurelius's logic to the question implies that repentance is required only if the right action—in this case, having a glass of wine—could be considered a good thing. But the best we could say about the glass of wine is that it would be a nice thing, but never good. Pleasure is never good or useful in the Stoic sense.

Repentance is a kind of self-reproof for having neglected something useful;[3] but that which is good must be something useful, and the perfect good person should look after it.[4] But no one would ever repent of having refused any sensual pleasure. Pleasure then is neither good nor useful.[5]

—VIII:10

1 Aurelius is stating something that is objectively obvious but perhaps never subjectively so, especially to a non-Stoic. If we experience great pain, we will either endure the pain and survive, or the pain will consume us and we will die. While we may prefer the former, death is at most no more than an inconvenience for the Stoic. This seemingly cold either-or dichotomy is intended to reinforce the Stoic belief that pain and death are never the things to fear. For most people, severe pain can be greatly exacerbated by the accompanying fear or panic that they might also die. It is this that troubles people most of all.

2 This is the classic Stoic response to hardship and pain. Notice that Aurelius never claims to make pain disappear; as a frontline military commander on campaign, Aurelius witnessed many examples of extreme pain. The object of the meditation is never to allow pain to erase our capacity for reason. The advice is sage, for in truth our ability to reduce pain (for example, to help prevent going into shock) or to address its root cause requires that we keep our wits. And we will keep our wits if we are able to alter our opinion about the pain. A modern sage might capture Aurelius's advice with the phrase, *do not panic, you have nothing to fear.* A Stoic soldier on the battlefield could whisper this to a mortally wounded comrade—and mean it.

3 Evil is any action contrary to reason. Pain may be bad in a colloquial sense, but pain as pain is simply a physical sensation. Pain may be important for physical survival (it informs us that the body or one of its organs is under some internal or external attack) and preferred, in this case, over having no pain. But, all things considered, no physical sensation should ever impinge on our happiness, which is an internal state depending only on virtue.

☐ Rising above Pain

Everything that happens either happens in such a way as you are formed by nature to bear it, or as you are not formed by nature to bear it. If, then, it happens to you in such way as you are formed by nature to bear it, do not complain, but bear it as you are formed by nature to bear it. But if it happens in such a way as you are not formed by nature to bear it, do not complain, for it will perish after it has consumed you.[1] Remember, however, that you are formed by nature to bear everything. It depends only on your own opinion to make anything that happens to you endurable and tolerable, by thinking that it is either your interest or your duty to do this.[2]

—X:3

Pain is either an evil to the body—then let the body say what it thinks of it—or to the soul; but it is in the power of the soul to maintain its own serenity and tranquility, and not to think that pain is an evil. Every judgment and movement and desire and aversion is within, and no evil ascends so high.[3]

—VIII:28

4 Epicurus was a Greek philosopher (c. 341–270 BCE). He maintained that pleasure was the purpose of all action. Although Epicurean philosophy was a rival to Stoicism, Aurelius as emperor established a school for Epicurean philosophy in Athens along with three others (Stoic, Platonic, and Aristotelian schools), all on an equal footing. This gesture was thoroughly consistent with the Stoic position on and toleration of freedom of expression.

Stoicism never viewed itself as a religion. It was a philosophy and used philosophical methods. As a philosophical system, it recognized that competing systems engaged in the same kinds of activity. Aurelius also recognized that many of the conclusions of the Stoics were drawn from arguments advanced in these rival schools over the four-hundred-year history of Stoicism that had preceded Aurelius and his *Meditations*. Although these schools held rival conclusions about the nature of reality, they respected each other. They also pursued opportunities to engage in open inter-philosophical debate and dialogue—a tradition already well established in the ancient world before Aurelius founded these schools. An example of how this worked is seen in this meditation. It was Epicurus, who was not a Stoic, who reinforced the Stoic position on pain, with his conclusion that "pain is neither intolerable nor everlasting, if you bear in mind that it has its limits, and if you add nothing to it in imagination."

5 In advocating that we retire into the mind, Aurelius is actually recommending meditation (over medication) as a form of pain management. The meditative process the Stoic advocates is not the same technique we might imagine employed in various Eastern traditions, although the insights garnered in the process might be similar. A Stoic retires into the mind not to empty the mind but to engage reason. The objective of meditation is intellectual activity divorced from the interferences and compulsions of bodily desires and fears.

The exercise, when applied to pain management, may not eliminate the pain, but it will allow us to see pain for what it really is: something that can either be endured or something that might consume

(continued on page 98)

In every pain let this thought be present, that there is no dishonor in it, nor does it make the governing intelligence worse, for it does not damage the intelligence either so far as the intelligence is rational or so far as it is social. Indeed in the case of most pains let this remark of Epicurus aid you, that pain is neither intolerable nor everlasting, if you bear in mind that it has its limits, and if you add nothing to it in imagination ....[4]

—VII:64

About pain: The pain which is intolerable carries us off; but that which lasts a long time is tolerable; and the mind maintains its own tranquility by retiring into itself, and the ruling faculty is not made worse. But the parts which are harmed by pain, let them, if they can, give their opinion about it.[5]

—VII:33

us. Whatever the case, the outcome is what nature intends for us—it will be according to nature, and nature is fundamentally beneficent. Once we take this step and adapt this attitude toward pain, the mind will be free to take on the things that are really important for us— namely, engaging in virtue. In the worst case, learning how to bear pain with nobility would be seen as virtuous and a source of peace and tranquility for the Stoic.

6 | This moving and powerful reflection on duty captures a great deal of the nobility of the Stoical stance toward life, pain, and death. Although the advice may appear unfeeling (in fact, it is unfeeling), the practical benefits of such a stance are enormous. We have duties in life, and there are many instances where we must sacrifice pleasure or comfort to do justice in the world. The sentiment here is echoed in the last three lines of the celebrated poem "Stopping by Woods on a Snowy Evening" by Robert Frost (1874–1963): "The woods are lovely, dark and deep, / But I have promises to keep, / And miles to go before I sleep, / And miles to go before I sleep."

✦ | For Aurelius, our first duty is always to others. But duty requires sacrifice. In an extreme, we may be required to sacrifice our life. But as this meditation reminds us, the duties associated with virtue may require that we forgo pleasure, comfort, food, sleep, money, and reputation. The places and situations demanding such sacrifices are varied. But whether these are the deprivations of a single parent, or the seventy-hour workweek of a struggling professional, the satisfaction and peace we obtain—if those activities are motivated by virtue—is sufficient reward, and can be achieved in practice through the application of meditative techniques described in more detail in part 6, "The Method of Stoicism."

Let it make no difference to you whether you are cold or warm, if you are doing your duty; and whether you are drowsy or satisfied with sleep; and whether ill-spoken of or praised; and whether dying or doing something else. For it is one of the acts of life, this act by which we die: it is sufficient then in this act also to do well what we have in hand.[6]

—VI:2

1 From the perspective of a twenty-first-century youth-oriented culture, this passage might read as a lead-in to a commercial for an anti-wrinkle cream, or a dieting program, or a geriatric medication. For Aurelius, aging and disease are evidence of the unavoidable and beautiful operations of nature. Because each of us is firmly embedded in nature, the dissolution and decay of our bodies are seen as manifestations of the divine character of natural law. The physical alterations our bodies experience may not seem beautiful in a classical sense. But the law producing those changes—the active intelligence of nature—is an immutable template for happiness, tranquility, and peace.

2 This is a form of taking stock in Stoic terms. None of the non-virtuous routine things we do in life has any bearing on our happiness; only virtue can make us happy. Death, therefore, deprives us of nothing important. However, the virtue we accomplish does not end with death because the good we do, no matter how small, is an essential element in a sequence of acts that connects each of us to every other human being. Our death, therefore, does not deprive the universe, because the good we do will live on as a necessary element in the social fabric of humanity. In a sense, the good that we do in our lives is what we were meant to do, and the totality of what we were meant to do. That awareness is sufficient to make us happy. Death itself is simply one of those routine things that must happen to everyone. We do not become unhappy when we die; we simply cease to exist. Therefore, even death is not a deprivation; death is necessary and according to nature.

3 Satisfaction for a Stoic is expressed as the serenity or tranquility that comes with virtue. Aurelius implies here that we cannot measure the value of serenity in the way we might measure pleasure or wealth or time. For example, we can't bank serenity or save it up for a rainy day. Serenity is a state of being, and states of being are not evaluated by the calculus of pleasure or measures of time. We are happy when we are, and when we die we cease to exist. It matters not how long we are happy but only that we are happy.

☐ Aging and Death

Turn the body inside out, and see what kind of thing it is;
and when it has grown old, what kind of thing it becomes,
and when it is diseased.[1]

—VIII:21

Often on the occasion of anything that you do, pause and
ask yourself if death is a dreadful thing because it deprives
you of this.[2]

—X:29

Be not dissatisfied then that you must live only so many
years and not more; for as you are satisfied with the amount
of substance which has been assigned to you, so be content
with the time.[3]

—VI:49

4 For Aurelius, these observations about how "perishable" and transient things are show us that the values we normally attach to life (pleasure, pain, fame, and the opinion of others) are meaningless phantoms and that these are also subject to dissolution and extinction.

5 For Aurelius, death is tinged with sweetness. Death is integral to and conducive of the nature we are fated to emulate. In embracing death, we merge back into the intelligence from which we spring.

6 This is a Stoic version of reductionism applied to death. It suggests that the physical organization of the material world, including living things, can be represented as the sum of its parts. This seemingly mechanistic scientific perspective of the universe does not so clearly extend to the ways in which Aurelius describes the active component of the universe, *Logos* or reason.

While Stoics do describe *Logos* and normal matter as intermixed in various ways, the nature of that mixing is never very clear. A modern Stoic might understand the ancient concept of *Logos* as predicting the physical force fields that modern physics uses to explain the interactions of matter. Electric, magnetic, nuclear, and gravitational forces attract or repel particles of ordinary matter, but the actual forces are themselves not thought of as composed of material particles. While there are particles involved in the *active* exchange of those forces (photons, gluons, etc.), their properties differ substantially from those of ordinary matter. Ancient Stoics might see these modern forces as the "finer" material they envisage as comprising the active principle of nature. Whatever the similarities, Stoics imagine *Logos* as a kind of constant or conserved property in nature that offers comfort around the idea of death. We as humans might lose our distinctness as individuals when we die, but our vital principle—derived as it is from *Logos*—will never die. We received this as a loan from nature when we were born, and we give it back to nature when we die. The *Logos* we return to nature remains to be reused in new ways and for new purposes.

How quickly all things disappear, in the universe the bodies themselves, but in time the remembrance of them; what is the nature of all sensible things, and particularly those which attract with the bait of pleasure or terrify by pain, or are noised abroad by vapory fame; how worthless, and contemptible, and sordid, and perishable, and dead they are—all this it is the part of the intellectual faculty to observe.[4] To observe too who these are whose opinions and voices give reputation; what death is, and the fact that, if you look at it in itself, and by the abstractive power of reflection resolve into their parts all the things which present themselves to the imagination in it, you will then consider it to be nothing else than an operation of nature; and anyone who is afraid of an operation of nature is a child. This, however, is not only an operation of nature, but it is also a thing which conduces to the purposes of nature. To observe too how you come near to the ruling intelligence, and by what part of you, and when this part of you is so disposed.[5]

—II:12

Death is such as germination is—a mystery of nature, a composition out of the same elements, and decomposition into the same; and altogether not a thing of which anyone should be ashamed, for it is not contrary to the nature of a reasonable animal, and not contrary to the reason of our constitution.[6]

—IV:5

7 The feeling of futility in attaining Stoic happiness reminds us of a Christian parallel on a question of salvation. In Mark 10:25, Jesus says: "It is easier for a camel to go through the eye of a needle than for someone who is rich to enter the kingdom of God." The point in both passages is that salvation (for a Christian) or serenity (for a Stoic) demands that we abandon false values such as wealth (the Christian example) or pleasure and fame (the Stoic example) for truth (the Christian example) and justice (the Stoic example).

8 Described as such, death has a certain appeal. Of the four processes mentioned, only one, the discursive movements of the thoughts, is under the control of reason. The three others—the cessation of the impressions through the senses, the pulling of the strings that move the appetites, and the service to the flesh—are all sources of pleasure and pain. The Stoic take-it-or-leave-it attitude toward these three means that their cessation is really no reason for anxiety. If anything, the end of these is also the end of temptation. While the loss of the discursive movement of thoughts might be a source of concern, this personal loss is really a gain in the Stoic universe. The reasoning principle in us is not degraded at death—it is simply released from the shackles of the body, where its essence is available once again for the service of nature. This knowledge should be a source of joy within an ethos that values and loves nature over the love of self.

9 This strange and cool recitation of Stoic factuality informs us that death is a reordering and a renewal, as well as a termination and a silencing of the self. Our death is according to nature. The nature Aurelius intuitively appreciates is one in accord with the principle of the conservation of mass and energy. When we die, our very atoms don't disappear but become the building blocks for other things as they are created.

You will soon die, and you are not yet simple, not free from disturbances, nor without suspicion of being hurt by external things, nor kindly disposed towards all; nor do you yet place wisdom only in acting justly.[7]

—IV:37

Death is a cessation of the impressions through the senses, and of the pulling of the strings that move the appetites, and of the discursive movements of the thoughts, and of the service to the flesh.[8]

—VI:28

That which has died falls not out of the universe. If it stays here, it also changes here, and is dissolved into its proper parts, which are elements of the universe and of yourself. And these too change, and they murmur not.[9]

—VI:18

10 There is no personal afterlife, in the religious sense, in Stoic philosophy. However, there is also no certainty around what happens to consciousness after death. The passive material body will dissolve, but the
active elements of consciousness and reason may or may not transform
into some other living form. Stoic philosophy was (and still is) grounded
on real facts about the world. As far as Aurelius is concerned, on matters such as these, the jury is out. There might, indeed, be some sort
of role for consciousness after death, but whatever that might be, it
would be unrelated to the life we have now, and it is never represented
in any way as either a reward or a punishment. The reward for living a
life of virtue is the joy of happiness here and now; the punishment for
vice is loneliness and despair.

He who fears death either fears the loss of sensation or a different kind of sensation. But if you shall have no sensation, neither will you feel any harm; and if you shall acquire another kind of sensation, you will be a different kind of living being and you will not cease to live.[10]

—VIII:58

11 Aurelius uses soul—*psyche* ("mind" in Greek)—as a synonym for reason. The Stoic soul has a material basis. The meaning should not be confused with the religious notion of the soul as a nonmaterial spirit.

There is a celebratory tone in the praise Aurelius expresses for the seasons of one's life. The Stoic treatment of nature and her operations is always done with tender reverence. There is also a curious analogy here between birth (coming out of the womb) and death (falling out of the envelope of life). Death is treated as if it were a rebirth. It is seen not as a rebirth of the self, but rather as a rebirth of the constituent parts that recycle into the cosmic pool and become available for new roles as different things. We explore this theme more closely in part 7, "Stoicism and the Environment."

12 The tone in this part of the passage is rather pessimistic about the vast mass of vulgar humanity whose principles are such that we might be relieved by death if only to be removed from their company. The purpose of this is to help us in reconciling death. There is no place in Stoicism for a withdrawal from, or to be offended by, or for any elitist display of disdain toward others. As Aurelius noted here, we have a duty to care for and bear with immoral people gently.

13 Aurelius is addressing those who might prefer life over death. Aurelius admits that one reward for living a good life—its joy—must be in sharing that life with those who share our principles. But even this he notes is lacking in the real world, where the discordance of most of those around us compels us to pray for a quick death.

Do not despise death, but be well content with it, since this too is one of those things which nature wills. For such as it is to be young and to grow old, and to increase and to reach maturity, and to have teeth and beard and gray hairs, and to beget, and to be pregnant and to bring forth, and all the other natural operations which the seasons of your life bring, such also is dissolution. This, then, is consistent with the character of a contemplative human being, to be neither careless nor impatient nor contemptuous with respect to death, but to wait for it as one of the operations of nature. As you now wait for the time when the child shall come out of the womb, so be ready for the time when your soul shall fall out of this envelope.[11] But if you require also a vulgar kind of comfort which shall reach your heart, you will be made best reconciled to death by observing the objects from which you are going to be removed, and the morals of those with whom your soul will no longer be mingled. For it is no way right to be offended with those around you, but it is your duty to care for them and to bear with them gently; and yet to remember that your departure will be from men and women who do not have the same principles as yourself.[12] For this is the only thing, if there be any, which could draw us the contrary way and attach us to life, to be permitted to live with those who have the same principles as ourselves. But now you see how great is the trouble arising from the discordance of those who live together, so that thou may say, *Come quick, O death, lest perchance I, too, should forget myself.*[13]

—IX:3

14 The meditation offers compelling and gentle observations about the distinct periods of a human life. To see these periods and the changes we undergo as a series of deaths is comforting to anyone near the end of life.

Termination of activity, cessation from movement and opinion, and in a sense their death, is no evil. Turn your thoughts now to the consideration of your life, your life as a child, as a youth, your adult life, and your old age, for in these also every change was a death. Is this anything to fear? Turn your thoughts now to your life under your grandfather, then to your life under your mother, then to your life under your father; and as you find many other differences and changes and terminations, ask yourself, *Is this anything to fear?* In like manner, then, neither is the termination and cessation and change of your whole life a thing to be afraid of.[14]

—IX:21

5 □ Stoicism and the Mind

1 Aurelius is fond of using the fountain as an image of the mind or soul. The flow of reason is forever renewed when the mind is properly attended and attuned to good.

2 Aurelius alternately refers to the human mind as the ruling faculty or simply reason. The mind may act autonomously, but it is also distilled from (or a node in) the ruling intelligence of the universe (*Logos*). Stoics sometimes referred to the extended mind as a world-soul and the individual mind as a particular soul.

Ralph Waldo Emerson (1803–1882) revived the idea of a world-soul or "Over-soul" in his 1841 essay of the same name. In the essay, he refers to the Over-soul as that "within which every man's particular being is contained and made one with all other." Emerson was a lifelong devotee of the writings of the Roman Stoic Seneca, but his concept of Over-soul was likely influenced more by Hindu philosophy than by Stoicism, although the functional similarities among all three concepts are intriguing. Among these, the Stoic *Logos* or world-soul is unique in its physical or corporeal (material-based) nature. In no sense is *Logos* outside of nature.

In Stoicism, when we are morally good our connections to the universal ruling intelligence bring us into alignment with the destiny of the universe. Entering into the ruling faculty of other human beings (and reciprocally allowing others to enter ours) is more than a casual suggestion. It is our duty to cooperate with others socially in realizing our destiny.

The process of entering into someone's ruling faculty is nothing mystical; rather, Aurelius means to achieve this using dialectic (logical argument). This involves the reciprocal and open exchange of ideas, through the use of logic-based critical thinking, writing, reading, and discourse, involving our powers of reason. It is important that the process is not contaminated by prejudice, self-interest, hidden agendas, or other ulterior motives. What may appear to be discourse in the modern context—in a political process, for example—is often motivated by a desire for power. For Aurelius, this would not qualify as valid discourse. We will look at this process more closely in part 6, "The Method of Stoicism."

☐ The Supremacy of Reason

Look within. Within is the fountain of good, and it will ever bubble up, if you will ever dig.[1]

—VII:59

Enter into every person's ruling faculty; and also let all others enter into yours.[2]

—VIII:61

3 Stoicism as a philosophy began with Zeno of Citium (see also the Introduction). But Stoics regard themselves as the legitimate heirs of the philosophy of Socrates (470–399 BCE) and present Socrates as their consummate exemplar (see also the Introduction).

4 Stoicism as a philosophy emphasizes the priority of the mind over sense impression and recognizes the interests of humanity over the interest of the individual.

5 This passage offers a succinct summary of what it means to be morally good. The mind rules over appetite and desire, and all physical senses should be subordinated to the mind. The mind is also coincident with the ruling intelligence of the universe and in sympathy with the individual minds of every human being. For Stoics, virtue is the only good, but virtue must be in accord with the laws of nature and comply with the social and political goals of the world community.

The practical good Aurelius refers to here depends on understanding nature. The laws of nature (determined from observations) and the ethics derived from an intelligent interpretation of those laws are found only through study and discourse. The methods of Stoicism were laid down in ancient texts, but our understanding of nature evolves with experience. We must uncover the laws of nature to understand virtue. In contrast, the ethical guidelines for many of the great world religions are revealed, in many instances, in the various wisdom literatures (such as the Bible). A Stoic, however, needs to examine the world carefully and rationally before making judgments.

6 The ancient Greek aphorism to "know yourself" is captured here in Stoic terms. Self-knowledge was long seen as a means to control any and all pleasures that might deter us from the contemplative life, or the life of the mind. Knowing yourself means knowing your mind. The body and its appetites really have nothing to do with who you really are. Using our reason, we are able to control the body and its appetites to ensure that these do not interfere with the mind.

Is anything better than the reason which is planted in you, which has subjected to itself all your appetites, and carefully examines all impressions, and, as Socrates[3] said, has detached itself from the persuasions of the senses, submitted itself to the gods, and cares for humanity?[4] Do you not find everything else smaller and of less value than this? Yield to nothing else, for as soon as you diverge, you will be distracted and no longer be able to give the preference to this good thing which is your proper possession and your own. For it is not right that anything of any other kind, such as reputation, or power, or enjoyment of pleasure, should compete with that which is rationally and politically or practically good.[5]

—III:6

The reason that governs knows what its own disposition is, and what it does, and on what material it works.[6]

—VI:5

7 Stoicism is a communal philosophy with cosmopolitan appeal. Its method is not restricted to an educated elite; anyone with a right disposition is able to engage its tenets. Stoics must consider whom they are addressing and communicate clearly and appropriately. Like a good architect or physician, Stoics should never be secretive about the governing principles of their craft. To accommodate the listener, Stoics will avoid talking down to people by carefully avoiding difficult or obscure language. However, like architects and physicians, Stoics should never compromise the fundamental principles and rules of their own reason.

8 The personal universe of the Stoic is one of constant movement and change. This continuous unfolding operates at the level of both the individual mind and the ruling intelligence of the universe. Whether this animating principle is identified as *Logos*—or in more modern terms as some (still undiscovered) unified field of modern physics (proposed originally by Albert Einstein)—the animating principle for both ancients and moderns is dynamic. It is never still or passive. Stoics view this dynamic principle as a fundamental fact about the nature of the world. The good life for the Stoic is a life of virtue. That means living in accordance with the active principle of nature. A Stoic may be tranquil and serene, but is always engaged. Mental numbness is not in accord with the dynamic facts of nature. Nevertheless, not all mental activity is virtuous—some actions may be contrary to nature.

9 My mind and the mind of my neighbor flow from and are also part of the ruling intelligence of the universe. There seems to be a contradiction here. Although the ruling intelligence is good by nature, individuals are able to act irrationally. But it is this apparent imperfection within the ruling intelligence that enables free will. If irrational behavior were not possible, we would be forever slaves to the ruling intelligence. This would eliminate any possibility of free will. Without freedom, we would be unhappy (or in some state of unconscious bliss) and therefore incapable of any self-actuated virtue.

Do you not see how experts accommodate themselves up to a certain point to those who are not skilled in their craft—nevertheless the experts cling to the basic principles and rules of their art and will never abandon these? Would it not be strange if the architect and the physician had more respect for the principles of their own professions than we for our own reason, which is common to us and to nature?[7]

—VI:35

Not in passivity, but in activity lie the evil and the good of the rational social animal, just as his virtue and his vice lie not in passivity, but in activity.[8]

—IX:16

Hasten to examine your own ruling faculty and that of the universe and that of your neighbor: your own that you may make it just, and that of the universe, that you may remember of what you are a part; and that of your neighbor, that you may know whether she has acted ignorantly or with knowledge, and that you may also consider that her ruling faculty is akin to yours.[9]

—IX:22

[✦] There is an interesting Judeo-Christian parallel on the origin of free will. One interpretation of the allegory of Eden in Genesis 2–3 is that humanity became fully human when Eve tasted the forbidden fruit from the Tree of the Knowledge of Good and Evil. In such a reading, this willed choice to defy the creator God can be interpreted as the first act of free will and the birth of reason, and Eve is the first redeemer, just as in Stoicism *Logos* may be viewed as redeeming humanity by permitting vice. In both situations, the choice was to forsake the attractive lure of slavery to the false and unreasonable gods of inauthenticity, falsehood, and addiction.

[10] This passage refers to the capacity of the rational human soul or reason to embrace and to comprehend all of nature, in both space and time. Reason is able to do this because it is part of a larger whole, the universal intelligence. Because we have this extraordinary power, we are able to understand nature and its laws, including the "periodical renovation of all things," an allusion to the Stoic theory that the universe undergoes cyclical re-births.

[11] This is the Stoic version of the principle of an all-knowing God. The Judeo-Christian God is no less all-knowing. We read in Proverbs 15:3, "The eyes of the Lord are in every place, keeping watch on the evil and the good." In Job 34:21–22, we learn, "For his eyes are upon the ways of mortals, and he sees all their steps. There is no gloom or deep darkness where evildoers may hide themselves."

The ruling intelligence of Stoicism is no less observant than the God of the Bible, but the consequences and conditions differ. For the Stoic, the all-knowing principle is part and parcel of what we are; the ruling faculty of the individual and the universal ruling faculty are made of the same stuff, not a deity to worship or placate. There is another important difference: evildoers are never punished. The motivation for Stoics is instead based on the positive direction to "see yourself [as governed by a ruling intelligence, and] you will rid yourself of much trouble." Lastly, the all-knowing and powerful patriarchal judge of biblical tradition is represented by Aurelius in other passages as a loving and cooperative mother who is eager to teach.

[The rational soul] traverses the whole universe, and the surrounding vacuum, and surveys its form, and it extends itself into the infinity of time, and embraces and comprehends the periodical renovation of all things.[10]

—XI:1

The ruling intelligence sees the ruling principles of all men and women bared of material cover and rind and impurities. The intelligence within you flows into your body from the ruling intelligence of the universe. If you see yourself in this way, you will rid yourself of much trouble. For whoever has little regard for the poor flesh which envelops the body, surely will not be troubled by a desire for fame and fortune.[11]

—XI:2

1 Aurelius maintains that what is good is also beautiful. It is interesting that his list of good things includes the lyre and knife—indicating that human artifacts can qualify as beautiful. These things are creative, useful, and purposeful works of human intelligence. As such, these things are more than simply works of art. For Aurelius, there is a difference. Works of art such as paintings or statues are examples of mimesis, imitations of real things, and therefore less authentic than the original. A fine painting or a statue may be helpful if it inspires us to virtue, but works of art are never good or beautiful as such.

For Aurelius, the only real good is virtue, and virtue is beautiful. Virtue does not improve when praised, or worsen if criticized. The vulgar (non-virtuous people) may call material things beautiful, but for Aurelius those are morally neutral. In a similar fashion, offering or expecting praise does not make something better. It is fine to encourage people to be virtuous, but praise itself is morally neutral. Aurelius's comments are directed to those who offer praise for irrelevant attributes such as fame, material possessions, dress, good looks, or health. Today, we might characterize this as feeding the ego, but ego is a modern concept developed by Sigmund Freud (1856–1939) and situated in Freud's conception of self. The Stoic would view Freud's ego as an emotional quality and therefore as something we might notice but never feed. Any need this ego might have to be fed would be seen as a false opinion. The real self to the Stoic is located in our ruling principles, and something we share in common with all of humanity.

☐ Supreme Beauty

Everything that is in any way beautiful, is beautiful in itself, and terminates in itself, not having praise as part of itself. Neither worse than nor better is a thing made by being praised. I affirm this also of the things which are called beautiful by the vulgar, for example, material things and works of art. That which is really beautiful has no need of anything; not more than law, not more than truth, not more than benevolence or modesty. Which of these things is beautiful because it is praised, or spoiled by being blamed? Is such a thing as an emerald made worse than it was, if it is not praised? Or gold, ivory, purple, a lyre, a little knife, a flower, a shrub?[1]

—IV:20

We ought to observe also that even the things which follow after the things that are produced according to nature contain something pleasing and attractive. For instance, when bread is baked some parts are split at the surface, and these parts which thus open, and have a certain fashion contrary to the purpose of the baker's art, are beautiful in a manner, and in a peculiar way excite a desire for eating. And again, figs, when they are quite ripe, break open; and in the ripe olives the very circumstance of their being near

(continued on page 125)

2 This earthy passage offers a reflection on the original version of the modern proverb, "Beauty is in the eye of the beholder." Aurelius observes that when we have a deeper insight into the things produced in the universe we will see beauty also in the changes and operations of nature. Beauty is not reserved for youth or springtime. There is beauty in the split surface of baked bread, because it excites appetite. The changes nature brings are also beautiful, as are ripened figs, olives near rottenness, and mature wheat, as well as an old woman or an old man. So, too, is there beauty in the lion's eyebrows, the foam that flows from the mouth of wild boars, and the gaping jaws of wild beasts.

By noting these things, Aurelius reminds us that everything changes, and that these changes are the ways of nature and her beautiful and immutable laws, which will be apparent to anyone who is "truly familiar with nature and her works." Interestingly, he also observes that the respect for nature these perspectives bring allows us to see youthful beauty in new ways and with "chaste eyes." In other words, in understanding nature and its inherent beauty and goodness, we are better disposed to act in virtuous ways.

to rottenness adds a peculiar beauty to the fruit. And the wheat bending down, and the lion's eyebrows, and the foam which flows from the mouth of wild boars, and many other things—though they are far from being beautiful, if you should examine them severally—still, because they are consequent upon the things which are formed by nature, help to adorn them, and they please the mind; so that if you should have a feeling and deeper insight with respect to the things which are produced in the universe, there is hardly one of those which follow by way of consequence which will not seem to you to be in a manner disposed so as to give pleasure. And so you will see even the real gaping jaws of wild beasts with no less pleasure than those which painters and sculptors show by imitation; and in an old woman and an old man you will be able to see a certain maturity and comeliness; and the attractive loveliness of young persons you will be able to look on with chaste eyes; and many such things will present themselves, while not pleasing to everyone, but to you who have become truly familiar with nature and her works.[2]

—III:2

1 For a Stoic, anything that lies between virtue (good) and vice (evil) should be viewed with indifference. The opinion that pleasure or pain is good or bad is false. The mind has the capacity to reject, or at least withhold, those labels when we are tempted to attach them to the wrong things. False opinions disturb the soul. The only interest for the soul is virtue. It is in our power to deny attaching these values to pleasure, power, money, or pain—thereby leaving the judgments of the soul unperturbed.

2 This passage offers an example of extraordinary power. We have the capacity to eliminate harm by removing the opinion that we suffer. The Stoic maintains that we suffer only when we believe we are harmed. But the Stoic also maintains that the soul is immune from harm. Aurelius does not deny the experiences we normally call harmful. We do and will feel painful physical and emotional sensations. But it is false to call these sensations bad or harmful. Pain signals concern or caution and allows us to seek remedy, but it is certainly not harmful. Physical or emotional pain is no harm at all if we extinguish the opinion that these experiences are harmful to reason.

☐ False Opinion

It is in our power to have no opinion about a thing, and not to be disturbed in our soul; for things themselves have no natural power to form our judgments.[1]

—VI:52

Take away your opinion, and then there is taken away the complaint, "I have been harmed." Take away the complaint, "I have been harmed," and the harm is taken away.[2]

—IV:7

6 □ The Method of Stoicism

1 Who would you rather identify with, the town mouse scurrying about in an alien world despised by all, or the country mouse living within the realm of nature? Aurelius is offering us a choice with his simple metaphor. We can live in fear and pain as unhappy souls, or we can live in peace and tranquility. The metaphor breaks down here because mice, of course, do not make these choices rationally. They live wherever they happen to be. Human beings, however, can choose between alternatives because we have reason. But like the mouse, we are also endowed with animal drives and passions. However, those passions are secondary to reason, because for the Stoic it is in reason that our real humanness and true nature reside. In choosing to follow our animal passions over reason, we abandon our humanity.

The alternative, the path of reason, is according to nature. But the choice for reason requires learning and intelligence. We need to understand what this choice involves, and we need to learn how reason works. Reason, unlike animal instinct, is a human power, but its cultivation requires work and a method. If it is peace and tranquility we desire, the methods of Stoicism promise us a way to achieve these.

✦ The method of Stoicism involves three stages. First, in coming to know ourselves we must *accept* our fate and abandon any discontent with what nature has provided for us. We must also embrace the possibility that the things we ought to love (nature and its goodness) might be something other than the objects we normally embrace (pleasure, power, money, fame, and so on). Second, we must be willing to *examine* the fabric of nature by engaging in philosophy with the goal of understanding nature's laws. Third, we must commit to *act* in the world in accordance with those laws as we discover them. In other words, we must live the life of virtue. These three stages are hierarchical, three rungs on a ladder ascending toward a truth that, although only dimly perceived at first becomes more defined as we ascend higher.

☐ Living according to Nature

Think of the country mouse and of the town mouse, and of the alarm and trepidation of the town mouse.[1]

—XI:22

✦ The first rung on the Stoic ladder requires that we abandon all discontent and blame. We must fully and gratefully accept who and what we are by nature. We must accept our fate. In doing this, we need also to accept the possibility that there is more to life than animal desire and prepare ourselves to take whatever steps are required to acquire wisdom.

1 Aurelius tells us what we must do to acquire the wisdom we will require for happiness. Only through wisdom are we able to love what is good. Truth is never obvious when we feel that we have been hard done by, or when we feel that life has dealt us a bad hand. These bad attitudes translate into resentment and anger—against God, or other people, or at life in general. Few people so disposed are open to wisdom. But Aurelius advises that what we are, or have become, is what we were destined to be. We must accept this as fate and do so without regret. To express dissatisfaction with what we are is a mutilation of the whole. Accepting ourselves as we are is a necessary step on the road to wisdom.

☐ Accepting Our Fate

For two reasons then it is right to be content with that which happens to you; the one, because it was done for you and prescribed for you, and in a manner had reference to you, originally from the most ancient causes spun with your destiny; and the other, because even that which comes severally to every human being is to the power which administers the universe a cause of joy and perfection, even of the very continuance of things. For the integrity of the whole is mutilated, if you cut off anything whatever from the conjunction and the continuity either of the parts or of the causes. And you do cut off, as far as it is in your power, when you are dissatisfied, and in a manner try to put anything out of the way.[1]

—V:8

2 This fascinating passage suggests that there is no such thing as blame for the Stoic. This goes beyond accepting whatever hand is dealt to us by nature. We must also accept the consequences of actions done to us deliberately by others. Because such actions are done out of ignorance, there is no reason for blame. In a sense, they are accidental. For the Stoic, ignorance of the law *is* an excuse. The ignorance we observe in others also triggers a duty on our part to correct the errors in others that led to those wrongs.

3 In making a choice for reason we need to abandon all barriers that restrict reason. These include hypocrisy, exclusive self-regard, and any discontent with our lot in life. Aurelius says we are drawn to these because we are blind to reason and unprepared to accept what reason might reveal. If we fail to abandon these barriers, our lives will continue as before. Self-interest will be our guide; our actions will be clouded by carelessness; our thoughts will focus only on ourselves—all the while grousing and grumbling about our miserable lot in life. There will be no peace; there will be no relief.

4 A promontory is a peninsula that acts as a natural breakwater. Whatever the opposing forces, not only does the promontory refuse to yield, but it actually changes the character of the forces it encounters. Once we accept the promise of the redemptive power offered through the philosophical orientation of Stoicism (the promise of happiness and freedom), we will, like the promontory, be in a position to tame the fury of our addictions to pleasure and our compulsive avoidance of discomfort and pain: the false values (values contrary to nature) that threaten to inundate our lives.

5 If life is as Aurelius describes—without apparent meaning, brief, and inconsequential—then where can we look for direction? Life, as Aurelius tells us here, is filled with unremitting pessimism. The dark language is intentional. If life really is "a warfare and a stranger's sojourn," is there nothing we can do to be free? This bleak assessment of life compels us to cry out: what, then, Aurelius?

With respect to that which happens conformably to nature, we ought to blame neither nature, for nature does nothing wrong either voluntarily or involuntarily, nor others, for they do nothing wrong except involuntarily. Consequently we should blame nothing.[2]

—XII:12

And you will give yourself relief, if you do every act of your life as if it were the last, laying aside all carelessness and passionate aversion from the commands of reason, and all hypocrisy, and self-love, and discontent with the portion which has been given to you.[3]

—II:5

Be like the promontory against which the waves continually break, but it stands firm and tames the fury of the water around it.[4]

—IV:49

Of human life the time is a point, and the substance is in a flux, and the perception dull, and the composition of the whole body subject to putrefaction, and the soul a whirl, and fortune hard to divine, and fame a thing devoid of judgment. And, to say all in a word, everything which belongs to the body is a stream, and what belongs to the soul is a dream and vapor, and life is a warfare and a stranger's sojourn, and after fame is oblivion.[5]

(continued on page 137)

6 | The answer, as surprising and strange now as it must have been then, is philosophy! This is what we must do to see life in a new way, to continue our journey to serenity. The word *philosophy* is compounded from the Greek roots *philos* (love) and *sophia* (wisdom). To engage in philosophy is to love (or seek) wisdom (or truth). Wisdom is the thing the Stoic seeks, and a love of wisdom will inevitably occur if we seek it.

But we must look. And that—in the simplest possible way—is all that Aurelius is saying. This is the Stoic version of the active appeal to faith by Jesus in Matthew 7:7, "Ask, and it will be given to you; search, and you will find; knock, and the door will be opened for you." This Christian example promises us knowledge and understanding of spiritual truths through the faith that comes to us from asking, searching, and knocking. The Aurelian version of this idea promises wisdom, too. But this wisdom requires a more explicit intellectual process, and loving wisdom is where it begins.

7 | Acceptance, the first rung on the Stoic ladder, also requires that we be willing to begin this journey. In other words, we must be prepared to engage in philosophy, to love wisdom. What does this loving wisdom require of us? It will require focusing exclusively on reason, while preparing ourselves for what will come after this. The journey ahead will require us to rise above pains and pleasures by seeing these as the illusions they are. It will later require acting always with due deliberation and with honesty, remaining self-reliant, accepting unconditionally what life delivers—while waiting for death with grace and sublime joy. It seems a tall order!

What then is that which is able to conduct a human being? It is one thing and only one, philosophy.[6] But this consists in keeping the spirit within free from violence and unharmed, superior to pains and pleasures, doing nothing without purpose or falsely or with hypocrisy, or feeling the need of another's doing or not doing anything; and besides, accepting all that happens, and all that is allotted, as coming from thence, wherever it is, from whence you yourself came; and, finally, waiting for death with a cheerful mind, as being nothing else than a dissolution of the elements of which every living being is compounded. But if there is no harm to the elements themselves in each continually changing into another, why should a human being have any apprehension about the change and dissolution of all the elements? For these things are according to nature, and nothing is evil which is according to nature.[7]

—II:17

✦ This second rung in the Stoic method requires an examination of the world. The process involves intellect, and the goal is moral. We seek knowledge not for its own sake, or for utility, or out of curiosity. Rather, we examine the fabric of nature so that we may learn how to live according to nature. The Stoic believes that, rightly understood, knowing nature and her laws will guide us to happiness, by showing us how to be virtuous.

We discover those laws when we look for them. The motivation to continue with this inquiry is driven by a love that plays out as an irresistible attraction for the beauty and goodness we begin to perceive as nature reveals herself to us. Aurelius calls this second stage in the method of Stoic practice, philosophy. Stoicism is neither restrictive nor elitist in practice, but Stoics must be prepared to engage in this practice using whatever skills are allotted to them by nature.

1 From a student's perspective, Aurelius was an ideal teacher. He not only regarded teaching as a two-way street, but he was also patient and kind. Toleration is an important characteristic of Stoicism. We have a duty to learn and an equal duty to share our understanding with others. By the same token, we must appreciate that human ignorance is involuntary, whatever behaviors that ignorance triggers. The poetic language "blame yourself, or blame not even yourself," is deliberate. Literally it means to forgive ignorance, yes, but then to look at yourself (know yourself) before attempting to correct the errors of others. This comment parallels a New Testament direction on judging others. In Matthew 7:4, Jesus says, "Or how can you say to your neighbor, 'Let me take the speck out of your eye,' while the log is in your own eye?"

☐ Inquiry and the Practice of Philosophy

If a person is mistaken, instruct her kindly and show her the error. But if you are not able, blame yourself, or blame not even yourself.[1]

—X:4

2 The administrator of the universe is *Logos,* or the universal intelligence.

3 The relationship of nature to each of us is as mother to child. We are children of nature, and our mother is loving and benign. If we fail to see this within our limited moment of existence, we will never know the joy that can flow from the experience. To do this, Aurelius tells us we must at last perceive the law that governs all. This is a strong imperative—a command to know nature. We will do that, eagerly and tenderly, when we are motivated by love.

4 This extraordinary and beautiful passage reads like a manual in critical thinking. It teaches us how to organize our approach to the examination of all aspects of nature. The approach involves reductionism (tearing everything down into its base components) and synthesis (showing how everything relates to the whole). Both of these processes are guided by a consciousness that these exercises are designed for elevation of the mind and will guide us in all of our actions.

5 While it is a given that the root natural law in the "highest city" must be directed by fellowship with benevolence and justice, it is up to us as free citizens in this constantly mutating world to interpret this law and to reconcile our actions to the ever-changing vagaries of life.

You must now at last perceive of what universe you are a part, and of what administrator of the universe[2] your existence flows from, and that a limit of time is fixed for you, which if you do not use for clearing away the clouds from your mind, time will go and you will go, and it will never return.[3]

—II:4

Make for yourself a definition or description of the thing which is presented to you, so as to see distinctly what kind of a thing it is in its substance, in its bareness, in its complete entirety, and tell yourself its proper name, and the names of the things of which it has been compounded, and into which it will be resolved. For nothing is so productive of elevation of mind[4] as to be able to examine methodically and truly every object which is presented to you in life, and always to look at things so as to see at the same time what kind of universe this is, and what kind of use everything performs in it, and what value everything has with reference to the whole, and what with reference to man, who is a citizen of the highest city,[5] of which all other cities are like families; what each thing is, and of what it is composed, and how long it is the nature of this thing to endure which now makes an impression on me, and what virtue I have need of with respect to it, such as gentleness, compassion, truth, fidelity, simplicity, contentment, and the rest.

(continued on page 143)

6 Aurelius never loses sight of his objective: what virtues will these examinations enable, and in what ways? And, how will this knowledge make me more humane, faithful, simple, and content? Along the way, Aurelius is laying foundations for the study of science (physics, chemistry, biology) and the humanities in all of its branches, including psychology, sociology, history, political science, ecology, and ethics. But the overall objective is uncovering nature's design.

7 The language we use needs to move directly to the target, like an arrow. The language must be appropriate. This means a careful choice of words targeted to the understanding of the listener. Why *utilize* a technical term if *use* will convey the same idea, and do it plainly? For Aurelius, technical, florid, deceptive, or ignorant language alienates. This is always inappropriate in a community where every citizen has the right to participate in the search for truth. Inappropriate language draws attention to the supposed authority of the speaker over the subject of discourse. It is also an affectation—something intended to draw attention more to the speaker's erudition than to the idea at hand.

8 The examination of nature requires discussion, and discussion is a mutual affair. Listening skills are essential. It is not sufficient merely to look interested in what others say. Nor is it enough to hear what words are used. A good listener must try to understand what lies beneath the words. What meanings does the speaker intend to convey? To attend carefully to what others say requires discipline, confidence, and psychological insight. If the speaker is sharing her concerns with the listener, it is important to notice every nuance in the communication. It is not enough to look interested while simply rehearsing a response.

Listening in this way not only makes better friendships, but also cultivates true intimacy. This closeness comes from attempting to see an idea exactly as another sees it. This is what the Stoic tries to do in all her communications—something she believes is according to nature because the place where ideas live (in the mind, through reason) comes ultimately from the same universal source.

Wherefore, on every occasion you should say: this comes from nature; and this is according to the apportionment and spinning of the thread of destiny, and such-like coincidence and chance; and this is from one of the same stock, and a kin and partner, one who knows not however what is according to human nature. But I know; for this reason I behave towards him or her according to the natural law of fellowship with benevolence and justice. At the same time, however, in things indifferent I attempt to ascertain the value of each.[6]

—III:11

Speak both in the senate and to every person, who ever that may be, appropriately, not with any affectation: use plain discourse.[7]

—VIII:30

Accustom yourself to attend carefully to what is said by another, and as much as it is possible, be in the speaker's mind.[8]

—VI:53

9 Q. Junius Rusticus was one of Aurelius's early teachers and the most distinguished Stoic philosopher of his time. Rusticus once lent his own copy of the works of the Stoic Epictetus to the young Aurelius. He was later a frequent advisor on private and public matters when Aurelius was emperor.

10 What applies to critical speaking and listening in the examination of nature is equally important in critical reading. Aurelius says elsewhere that we must be in the speaker's mind. That advice applies equally to our reading skills. A superficial understanding occurs when grazing thoughtlessly and passively through a book while ignoring the mind of the writer, or the context of the ideas. Aurelius regards reading as an active process. When we read we engage in an imaginary conversation with the writer. That conversation is, in turn, a part of a larger conversation involving all of the other books we have read—even if the book's ideas oppose what we may believe, because this, too, is part of the examination.

11 Aurelius is amusing in his advice to reserve judgment of those "who talk overmuch." He detects, rightly, that over-talking or holding sway in conversations signifies an incapacity to listen, a disinterest in others, and more insightfully—if ironically—insecurity and ignorance on the part of the speaker.

From Rusticus[9] ... [I learned] to read carefully, and not to be satisfied with a superficial understanding of a book;[10] nor hastily to give my assent to those who talk overmuch.[11]

—I:7

+ The third rung in the Stoic method requires an activity called virtue. Happiness comes from living in accordance with nature's law. As we come to know nature, we come to understand the principles that must govern our actions. One of those principles is that all of our actions must be directed toward the interests of others and the community at large. This is what living according to nature requires. Actions that conform to these principles are called virtues.

1 Aurelius is fond of enumerating and prioritizing three Stoic principles. The first principle is that we are social beings. We are designed for altruism because we are all citizens of a larger design, comprising a world community.

2 The second principle is that the active aspect of nature is rational, and the rational is always superior to the animal. Our animal senses are nonetheless real and serve the purpose of informing the rational, but we should never confuse the animal in us with what we truly are.

3 The third principle is that as rational creatures we are deeply integrated within the perfect fabric of nature. When we know this about ourselves (by following systematically and honestly the methods outlined by Aurelius in these chapters), we will come to know the freedom that only comes from such perfection. In so doing, Aurelius claims that our actions will be freed from error or deception.

Whether this is an ideal that is truly possible in practice or merely approximated in the real world, only a true Stoic can say. But it is important to note that Aurelius uses the idea of error mainly to refer to our choices. We do not err if we choose to act with virtue. We do err if we reject virtue by acting contrary to nature. Likewise, Aurelius uses deception in the sense that we cannot be deceived that a virtue is really a vice, or vice versa.

☐ The Life of Virtue

The prime principle then in the rational constitution is the social.[1] The second principle is never to yield to the persuasions of the body, for it is the peculiar task of the rational and intelligent function to surround itself and never to be overpowered either by the activity of the senses or of the appetites—for both are animal; but the intelligent activity claims superiority and does not permit itself to be overpowered by the others. And with good reason, for it is formed by nature to use all of the senses.[2] The third thing in the rational constitution is freedom from error and from deception. Let then the ruling principle holding fast to these things go straight on, and it has what is its own.[3]

—VII:55

4 This passage underscores the importance of flexibility for the Stoic. Stoicism is not a system bound to any literal interpretations of a sacred scripture because there are no sacred scriptures. This is not a system constrained by the pronouncements of religious authorities because there are no religious authorities; no one—not even an emperor—is privileged. There is one law—the law of nature—and it is up to us to discover that law, and to act in accordance with nature following the dictates of our own reason and conscience.

Because we are bound together through reason, we are bound also to respect that the justifications we use for our actions can change. We ought to be free to alter our opinions and actions if offered a compelling argument developed from reason. But we should never alter an opinion or action because it appears pleasant or brings reputation.

You should always have these two rules in readiness; the one, to do only whatever the reason of the ruling and legislating faculty may suggest for your use; the other, to change your opinion, if there is anyone at hand who sets you right and moves you from any opinion. But this change of opinion must proceed only from a certain persuasion, as of what is just or of common advantage, and the like, not because it appears pleasant or brings reputation.[4]

—IV:12

7 □ Stoicism and the Environment

1 For Stoics, everything in nature is an offspring of a seed, or a seminal reason. These seeds may be analogous to biological seeds or spores, but Aurelius means something more. In his *Lives of the Eminent Philosophers,* the Greek Cynic philosopher Diogenes (c. 399–323 BCE), in writing about the ideas of the early Stoics, described these seeds as *spermatikoi logoi* (seeds of *Logos*). Aurelius offers no more detail than this.

✦ Biology was a primitive science in the second century, but the concept of the intermixing of active and passive principles (body and soul) in human beings can be presumed as something that occurs in the initial stage of life, in parallel with the religious concept of the soul entering the body. For the Stoic, this intermixing of active and passive principles occurs with everything in the natural world. Because the active principle is common to all things in nature, everything in nature shares its origin and derives its various traits ultimately from the universal intelligence. This commonality of origin is a bond uniting all of nature. For the Stoic, nature is a unity with a shared cosmic purpose and destiny. This idea contrasts with the Judeo-Christian idea of a nature separately created for the use and dominion of humanity.

2 Aurelius's use of the word *abuse* is clearly respectful; it is not intended to imply something improper or a misuse of nature in the modern sense. In a modern culture where nature is seen as something to be harnessed or used for human benefit, the word *abuse* might be reserved for the sense of mismanagement. But in Stoic culture, where all of nature is seen as emanating from the same source as the humans who must harvest its bounty in order to live, people are likely to be more respectful and thankful. This attitude is similar to the custom of giving thanks to the plant you are about to pluck, as practiced by North America's indigenous people.

☐ The Seeds of Logos

I go through the things which happen according to nature
until I shall fall and rest, breathing out my breath into that
element out of which I daily draw it in, and falling upon
that earth out of which my father collected the seed[1] and
my mother the blood, and my nurse the milk; out of which
during so many years I have been supplied with food and
drink; which bears me when I tread on it and abuse it for so
many purposes.[2]

—V:4

[1] For Aurelius, the nature of the whole is the universe in which the earth is a part, unified through an inseparable mixture of matter bound to a set of universal laws. Our nature is that we, too, are connected to the whole; we are rational beings distilled from the earth, which in turn is distilled from the whole.

[✦] According to philosopher Charles Taylor, a major consequence of abandoning the notion that we share common laws and values is individualism. This implies that what matters most in life is personal fulfillment. My beliefs and values come from within, and I have a right to carry out my life projects free from any interference from others. This perspective is usually referred to as "soft relativism." It maintains that all ways of being are equivalent and morality is however we define it subjectively. Soft relativism is used to reject anything and everything that transcends the self. This includes a wide range of things, such as the past, citizenship, religion, spirituality, solidarity, and, of course, the environment.

There is an environmental consequence when we abandon the idea of a common morality or a shared intelligence. This occurs when we substitute a new kind of reason that Taylor calls "instrumental reason." This means making rational decisions based exclusively on economic efficiency. Taylor argues that this is really a kind of fuzzy logic because it ignores real human values. Some would argue that the instrumentally guided directions our culture has taken in its industrial decisions over the past few centuries have brought us to the brink of global disaster. We have instrumentally reasoned our species to the edge of an abyss. For the first time in the few billion years that life has been working itself out here, the quality and quantity of solar radiation reaching the biosphere is changing, in a fundamental way. We are interfering with the worldwide system of water, land, and air, and doing this during an era in which global population is approaching ten billion people.

☐ The Sacredness of Nature

This you must always bear in mind, what is the nature of
the whole, and what is my nature, and how this is related to
that, and what kind of a part it is of what kind of a whole;
and that there is no one who hinders you from always
doing and saying the things which are according to the
nature of which you are a part.[1]

—II:9

2   This prayer is touching in its profound reverence for the sacredness of nature. Nothing in the tone suggests a need or desire to harness or dominate nature. Humanity is neither above nor below nature. We are deeply embedded in nature. There is no plea here for an abundant harvest or a calm sea or blue skies. There is no appeal for forgiveness from an avenging or vengeful nature. This prayer comes from a world that understands the fury of nature, but expresses no sense of worry or fear of what nature can bring. For Aurelius, nature is as benign in her fury as she is benign in her bounty. In a modern world facing possible cataclysmic consequences from climate change, adopting a more benign attitude toward nature could offer comfort and even remedy in the longer term. If it was alienation from nature that informed the industrial era's exploitation of Earth, then the concerns we face now may bring us closer to the attitudes toward nature held by our Stoic ancestors—attitudes that could end not only our estrangement but also teach us how to live within the constraints that nature wills.

Everything harmonizes with me, which is harmonious to you, O Universe. Nothing for me is too early nor too late, which is in due time for you. Everything is fruit to me which your seasons bring, O Nature: from you are all things, in you are all things, to you all things return.[2]

—IV:23

1 The one living being that has perception is *Logos*.

2 In 1979, the book *Gaia: A New Look at Life on Earth* by James Lovelock (b. 1919) proposed an ecological theory that modeled Earth as a complex "living" system, behaving *as if* it were a single organism with interacting components. It is a serious and respectable scientific hypothesis. Lovelock argues that the soil, water, and air on Earth are linked to the biosphere through feedback mechanisms that maintain the optimal conditions for life. It is no accident that the things essential for life, such as temperature, oxygen, soil salinity, and so on, stay within the necessary range of values for life. The biosphere works in ways to guarantee these ranges in values. The process is natural and unconscious. It simply manifests a higher order of systemic organization than do older theories about life on Earth. Those older theories suggest that life maintains itself on Earth because conditions just happen to be right—a fortunate accident.

There is little question that Aurelius would have embraced Lovelock's Gaia. Aurelius's proclamation of an ancient and universal Gaia ecology extends well beyond Earth. Aurelius regarded the entire universe as exhibiting organizational principles, and he had no reservation about referring to this system of organizational principles as "one living being." A scientist today would likely not go as far as Aurelius, but still might be tempted to agree that those unifying principles cooperate with one another *as if* they were orchestrated by "one living being."

☐ Cosmic Gaia and the Unity of Nature

Constantly regard the universe as one living being, having
one substance and one soul; and observe how all things
have reference to one perception, the perception of this
one living being;[1] and how all things act with one
movement; and how all things are the cooperating causes of
all things which exist; observe too the continuous spinning
of the web and the interconnections in all of its parts.[2]

—IV:40

3 | Mount Athos, or the Holy Mount as it is known today, is the center of Eastern Christian Orthodox monasticism, located on the Athonite peninsula in Macedonia in northeastern Greece. The area is one of outstanding natural beauty and is home to twenty monasteries, forming a semiautonomous monastic republic within modern Greece. In antiquity, Mount Athos was commonly referred to as a mountain of prodigious height.

4 | This passage reinforces the notion of the interconnectedness and scale of nature—the tiny place and role we play in nature's scheme. In a theme we have seen in other meditations, Aurelius directs us to see beauty not only in the things that are grand and beautiful but also in the after-products of those: "the lion's gaping jaws, and that which is poisonous, and every harmful thing, as a thorn, as mud." When we understand the connections and relationships in nature and how all things proceed from the same natural cause, we become aware of the unity and beauty in all of nature, including those things many would call harmful.

Asia and Europe are corners of the world: all the sea is a drop in the universe; Mount Athos[3] a little clod of the universe: all the present time is a point in eternity. All things are little, changeable, perishable. All things come from thence, from that universal ruling power either directly proceeding or by a sequence of causes. And accordingly the lion's gaping jaws, and that which is poisonous, and every harmful thing, as a thorn, as mud, are after-products of the grand and beautiful. Do not then imagine that they are of another kind from that which you do venerate, but form a just opinion of the source of all.[4]

—VI:36

1 The Stoic statement of ecological unity proclaims not only that nature is united and interconnected but also that those bonds are sacred.

✦ This Stoic attitude toward nature has technological implications. Technologies are products of reason. They can be developed either according to nature or contrary to nature. A Stoic approach would look to nature for leadership.

University of Victoria (British Columbia) engineering professor and hydrogen pioneer David Scott likes to draw on the example of a tree in a metaphor on how nature can inspire technology. The tree, says Scott, draws carbon dioxide from the air and water from the earth. The tree then extracts carbon from carbon dioxide, and hydrogen from water using solar energy—a natural technology called photosynthesis. The tree then reassembles carbon and hydrogen as leaf and branch. The after-product of this technology is the waste we call oxygen. All oxygen in the atmosphere is the waste of photosynthesis.

The most ubiquitous machine of the modern era, the automobile engine, offers an example of a technology that opposes nature, because it mimics nothing in nature. In fact, its design is contrary to nature. It has two inputs, gasoline from prehistoric trees and oxygen from air, which combine to release energy. Most of this energy is wasted as heat. The other wastes from this technology—carbon dioxide and other pollutants—contaminate and foul the biosphere.

If we are to work in accord with nature, it makes sense to develop technologies that harmonize with nature. The tree—seen as a technology—took several billion years to get right. There's no reason to reinvent the wheel—just copy the tree. The "according to nature" fuel-cell engine technology that this metaphor serves uses renewable energy sources to combine hydrogen—a fuel obtained by splitting water—with oxygen. The oxygen and hydrogen combine like chemicals do in plant cells. The output, electricity, is used for power. The after-product is pure water—where we started: a renewable, recyclable, and nonpolluting process. The metaphor of the tree as technology expresses a truth about how nature is organized and how we—as interconnected parts of nature—might organize ourselves, if we are to remain part of nature.

☐ Imitating Nature in Our Technologies

All things are implicated with one another, and the bond is holy; and there is hardly anything unconnected with any other thing. For things have been coordinated, and they combine to form the same universe. For there is one universe made up of all things, and one ruling intelligence who pervades all things, and one substance, and one law, one common reason in all intelligent animals, and one truth; if indeed there is also one perfection for all animals which are of the same stock and participate in the same reason.[1]

—VII:9

1 Love is central to Stoic philosophy and is the driving force not only in nature's realm but also in the quest for virtue. The desire behind love is often expressed as an upwardly directed striving impulse toward not only that which is beautiful but also that which is good. The souls of animals come from the same source as the souls of human beings and likewise are attracted in their own ways toward the same universal intelligence because they too are made of the same stuff.

2 Aurelius is likely referring to the herding or flocking instinct.

3 In human beings, the striving to express kinship through families, nations, and even a world community with its various alliances and bonds, expresses itself in a superior way. Those connections extend even in wars—in the battles themselves, which would be regarded as forms of instruction—and in the treaties and armistices that grow out of wars.

4 In the ancient worldview, the stars were believed to be very large bodies located at a vast distance from the earth. In spite of this, the stars appeared to move in unison in their nightly rotation from east to west. The motion was considered evidence of kinship in the superior (higher) realm of nature.

☐ Nature and Climate Change

Accordingly among animals devoid of reason we find swarms of bees, and herds of cattle, and the nurture of young birds, and in a manner, loves.[1] For even in animals there are souls, and that power which brings them together is seen to exert itself in the superior degree, and in such a way as never has been observed in plants nor in stones nor in trees.[2] But in rational animals there are political communities and friendships, and families and meetings of people; and in wars, treaties and armistices.[3] But in the things which are still superior, even though they are separated from one another, unity in a manner exists, as in the stars. Thus the ascent to the higher degree is able to produce a sympathy even in things which are separated.[4]

—IX:9A

5 Because we have free will, we have the capacity to deviate from the attractive mutual desire and inclination that serves as the bonding force (love) in every other realm of nature.

6 This is Aurelius's way of saying that "love conquers all." At the end of the day, nature will have its way.

+ This note of optimism from the past is comforting to the ears of moderns as we begin to address the problems of climate change. The words of Aurelius imply that our human nature and the nature that we have been abusing for so long are one and the same. The modern world has struggled to avoid this union since the beginning of the industrial age. But it is only intelligent animals who have forgotten this mutual desire and inclination between nature and humanity. At the dawn of the twenty-first century, we see that we have been caught and held by nature: glaciers are retreating; sea levels are rising; forests are disappearing; the climate is changing; we *are* feeling the heat—literally and figuratively. Aurelius would tell us now that our human nature is too strong for us to remain alienated from our source. He would also tell us that it *is* within our intellectual power to see this looming misfortune as an opportunity to restore the harmony between nature and humanity that is the basis of human purpose.

See, then, what now takes place. For only intelligent animals have now forgotten this mutual desire and inclination, and in them alone the property of flowing together is not seen.[5] But still though people strive to avoid this union, they are caught and held by it, for their nature is too strong for them; and you will see what I say, if you only observe.[6]

—IX:9B

8 □ The Practice of Stoicism

1 Why would Aurelius choose the wrestler's art as his simile for the art of life? What does this tell us about the struggle for success in life? For Aurelius, it is only the wrestler who is "ready and firm to meet onsets that are sudden and unexpected." The wrestler's art requires strength and cunning, as well as grace and balance. For the Stoic, the goal and end of life is virtue, the only good. But the path to virtue is strewn with trickery, deception, and falsehood, and navigating that path requires quick thinking, caution, and constant vigilance. The strength and cunning of the wrestler's art are analogues for the courage and wisdom required of the Stoic sage, and the cultivation of these is the goal of all meditation and prayer.

☐ Meditation, Prayer, and the Wrestler's Art

The art of life is more like the wrestler's art than the dancer's, in respect of this, that it should stand ready and firm to meet onsets which are sudden and unexpected.[1]

—VII:61

2   The tradition of prayer is central to Stoic activity. Prayers within many religious traditions involve an implicit conversation with a deity, often in the form of a request or a petition. Stoic meditation is no different, but these requests always take place within "this little territory of your own." The objective of Stoic prayer is rational freedom. Rational freedom resides in the mind, and is achieved by living according to nature through the practice of philosophy and contemplation. For the Stoic, rational freedom confers invincibility—the power to experience authentic joy through the practice of virtue. The only barrier for a Stoic to rational freedom is the internal opinion that externals will cause harm. Those externals include anything that can cause personal or social anxiety: job insecurities, troubled relationships, dissatisfactions with our talents or appearance, poor health, aging, terrorism, money problems, war, environmental decay, and death.

This list is the same as for anyone living in a troubled world. A Stoic will never say that any of these is irrelevant. But guided by meditation and self-reflection, the Stoic places these concerns in their proper place. The objective of the Stoic is to prevent the emotions from disabling our capacity to reason well—not through denial but through reevaluation.

Those things that are according to nature—aging, death, or dissatisfaction with what we are by nature—are beyond our control. The only healthy attitude around these is acceptance. It might be difficult for non-Stoics to accept these attitudes. But it is possible to think this way. Meditation and prayer is the vehicle the Stoic uses to cultivate this mind-set by reinforcing her understanding of nature and her place in it.

This then remains: Remember to retire into this little territory of your own, and above all do not distract or strain yourself, but be free, and look at things as a man or as a woman, as a human being, as a citizen, as a mortal. But among the things readiest to your hand to which you shall turn, let there be these, which are two. One is that things do not touch the soul, for they are external and remain immovable; but our disturbances come only from the opinion which is within. The other is that all these things, which you see, change immediately and will no longer be; and constantly bear in mind how many of these changes you have already witnessed. The universe is transformation: life is opinion.[2]

—IV:3

1 The art of living includes the work we do and the businesses we manage. The passage conveys the Stoic attitude toward work and even labor relations. Aurelius counsels us that our working life is a major part of our duty in the world. However humble that work may be, we should be content because the art we learn is part of nature's package and plan. It was designed for us for a reason and by reason. We ought also to work as diligently as we can, "with [our] whole soul." The duty around work carries a responsibility: never to exploit others (a management responsibility if our work is to direct others as an employer) or to be exploited (as an employee), "[make] yourself neither the tyrant nor the slave of any person."

2 This section covers a lot of ground. Particularly noteworthy is the expression of compassion for those who do wrong. This goes beyond loving our enemy. Aurelius wants us to understand that wrongdoers are not only kindred in body, but also truly kindred in spirit: they share with us the same origin in universal reason.

3 There is much Stoic wisdom in this colorful passage. Living in the world is a skillful art, more akin to that of the wrestler (see previous section) than that of the dancer. This requires cunning, strength, and wit. The world we labor in is full of challenges, trickery, and sometimes outright savagery as we contend with the "busy-body, the ungrateful, arrogant, deceitful, envious, unsocial." The wise person needs always to be mindful, not only of what is good (living with nature) and what is bad (living contrary to nature), but also that we are social by nature ("they are kindred to me") and connected by universal reason through a shared destiny that is realized only through cooperation, not competition. We must also recognize that the obstacles placed before us by others can never damage what is innately human in us (our reason)—"I can never be injured by any of them"— and that those obstructions are rooted in human ignorance, not malevolence. It is therefore our duty to correct and instruct, never to punish.

☐ Implications for Work and Business

Love the art, poor as it may be, which you have learned, and be content with it; and pass through the rest of life like one who has trusted nature with your whole soul and with all that you have, making yourself neither the tyrant nor the slave of any person.[1]

—IV:31

Begin the morning by saying to yourself, Today I shall meet with the busy-body, the ungrateful, arrogant, deceitful, envious, unsocial. All these things happen to them by reason of their ignorance of what is good and evil. But I who have seen the nature of the good—that it is beautiful, and of the bad—that it is ugly, and the nature of those who do wrong—that they are kindred to me, not only of the same blood or seed, but that they participate in the same intelligence and the same portion of the universal reason. I can neither be injured by any of them, for no one can fix on me what is ugly, nor can I be angry with my kin, nor hate.[2] For we are made for cooperation, like feet, like hands, like eyelids, like the rows of the upper and lower teeth. To act against one another then is contrary to nature; and it is acting against one another to be angry and to turn away.[3]

—II:1

4 Any work we perform in our capacity as human beings is appropriate and dignified insofar as that work is in accordance with the laws of nature. Work contrary to nature is not just inappropriate; it is also evil. As far as Aurelius is concerned, there is no hierarchy in work, any more than there is a hierarchy in nature's will. Everything we do in accordance with nature has significance because it is necessary in the plan of nature. As human beings, we can do only what we are assigned by nature to do, and what we have been assigned by nature to do is what we are meant to do. The only ambition proper for a human being is the ambition to live in accord with nature's will.

Can we be ambitious with regard to our work? Not if that ambition is tied to getting ahead for a self-serving purpose: power, reputation, or wealth. The only ambition appropriate for a Stoic is to serve others and to do that with virtue. Wealth, fame, and power may still come to someone with Stoic ambition. Aurelius himself was just such a man. He spent his life in serving others and did so with virtue. He was also wealthy, famous, and powerful.[1]

The labor which the hand or foot does is not contrary to
nature, so long as the foot does the foot's work and the
hand the hand's. So then your labor as a human being is not
contrary to nature, so long as it does the things of a human
being. If your labor is not contrary to your nature, it is not
an evil to you.[4]

—VI:33

5 Two important general elements of the Stoic attitude toward work survive in modern free-market economies. First, few companies or businesses survive if they are unprepared or fail to recognize that change—a critical idea in understanding nature for the Stoic—is inevitable. Second, individuals, new businesses, and entrepreneurs are expected to accept the idea that hard work and discomfort—something Stoics learn to accept without complaint—is necessary for long-term success.

The specific work ethic Aurelius proclaims in this passage would certainly meet the ethical standards expected from most employers today: love your job; do it for the common interest; focus exclusively on the job at hand; do it competently; and do it with good cheer. But the common interest for Aurelius is something greater than the idea "What is good for General Motors, is good for America."[2] For the Stoic, the common interest is the interest shared by both the worker and the rest of the human community, not just the interest of the company or country. This Stoic ethic around work transfers also to the environment (see part 7, "Stoicism and the Environment"). Such an ethic must be environmentally sound if it is simultaneously good for the common interest and done according to the plan of nature.

Work not unwillingly, nor without regard to the common interest, nor without due consideration, nor with distraction; nor let studied ornament set off your thoughts, and be not either a person of many words, or busy about too many things.... Be cheerful also, and seek not external help nor the tranquility which others give. A human being must stand erect, not be kept erect by others.[5]

—III:5

✦ This ten-step program is typical of the approach Aurelius brings to his method. This particular program is configured as an early exercise in "anger management" and dealing with people who have "offended" us. The exercise is intended to curb our emotional reactions in these situations and diffuse irrational responses to offensive acts or insults. But the exercise can also be generalized as a way of summarizing the Stoic stance toward the world. Aurelius presents us with these ten rules, paraphrased as follows:

1. Know yourself and understand your relationship to others.
2. Know others and study their foibles.
3. Recognize that ignorance in others is involuntary.
4. Acknowledge that you are essentially the same as others.
5. Motives are difficult to discern—never assume to know what these are.
6. Remember that life is short.
7. Recognize that actions by others never cause us harm—only our reactions do.
8. Acknowledge that pain stems from our anger over an action—never the action itself.
9. Educate the offender—the harm done is to him alone.
10. Expect offense—it is irrational not to.

1 *Know yourself and understand your relationship to others.* This first rule is the first step in all Stoic methodology. We must know ourselves, accept what we are, and understand where we stand in our relationship to others. In his own case, Aurelius is a leader and accepts without arrogance the fact that he was designed to be as a ram over the flock or a bull over the herd. Knowing yourself means knowing your mind and understanding the relationship between mind and body (see also the chapter, "On Knowing Yourself and 'Wolfish' Friendships").

2 *Know others and study their foibles.* The second rule follows from the first. Aurelius expects us to attend to the actions of others and to analyze them psychologically by understanding compulsions. Acting contrary to nature—as people who offend must do—is to act under the influence of self-interest or pride. People who mean to offend will build themselves up by putting us down. Understand this, and the offense will dissolve.

☐ A Ten-Step Program in Anger Management

If any have offended against you, consider first: What is my relation to others, and that we are made for one another; and in another respect, I was made to be set over them, as a ram over the flock or a bull over the herd. But examine the matter from first principles, from this: If all things are not mere atoms, it is nature which orders all things: if this is so, the inferior things exist for the sake of the superior, and these for the sake of one another.[1]

—XI:18A

Second, consider what kind of people they are at table, in bed, and so forth: and particularly, under what compulsions in respect of opinions they are; and as to their acts, consider with what pride they do what they do.[2]

—XI:18B

3 *Recognize that ignorance in others is involuntary.* The third rule is a consequence of the second. The classic "put-down" often plays out as an insult we find difficult to swallow. Aurelius's categories are as relevant now as they were in his age. No one, for example, likes to be unfairly called unjust, ungrateful, or greedy. But insults often happen in these ways, and we feel pained when we are unjustly accused. Aurelius advises us that the offender who says these things is usually acting from ignorance.

4 *Acknowledge that you are essentially the same as others.* In this fourth rule, Aurelius captures a sentiment expressed in the aphorism: "There but for the grace of God (or reason, in the Stoic case), go I." Aurelius reminds us here that we, too, are capable of acting wrongly. We, too, are capable of offense. We, too, have likely caused offense in the past.

5 We do not know and likely cannot know all of the mitigating circumstances around the actions of others. Always keep this in mind.

6 *Motives are difficult to discern—never assume to know what these are.* This fifth rule is the principle of toleration. Aurelius reminds us that human beings are complex; their motives are never clear; their intentions never at all obvious. Things are rarely as they seem. The anger we express toward the erratic driver of the car behind us may be misplaced. He may be a distraught parent rushing to the hospital to see his injured child.

7 *Remember that life is short.* This sixth rule is grounded in perspective. Life is brief, the universe is immense, and soon we will die. Don't sweat the small stuff.

Third, that if people do rightly what they do, we ought not to be displeased; but if they do not right, it is plain that they do so involuntarily and in ignorance. For as every soul is unwillingly deprived of the truth, so also is it unwillingly deprived of the power of behaving to each person according to his or her deserts. Accordingly, people are pained when they are called unjust, ungrateful, and greedy, and in a word wrongdoers to their neighbors.[3]

—XI:18C

Fourth, consider that you also do many things wrong, and that you are a person like others. And even if you do abstain from certain faults, still you have the disposition to commit them, though either through cowardice, or concern about reputation, or some such base motive, you do abstain from such faults.[4]

—XI:18D

Fifth, consider that you do not even understand whether people are doing wrong or not, for many things are done with a certain reference to circumstances.[5] And in short, a person must learn a great deal to enable passing a correct judgment on another's acts.[6]

—XI:18E

Sixth, consider when you are much annoyed or grieved, that human life is only a moment, and after a short time we are all laid out dead.[7]

—XI:18F

8 *Recognize that actions by others never cause us harm—only our reactions do.* The seventh rule helps us in resolving anger. The only thing that really ever will disturb us is the opinion we hold about the offense. But opinion is one of the things over which we have power. Withhold opinion, and the harm will disappear.

Suppose that because of favoritism the promotion you deserved is given to someone with far fewer qualifications than you. There is no question that this is unfair. You feel angry, resentful, and bitter. Over time, these feelings eat away at you and affect your job performance. Your reactions to the injustice are harming you. But anger, resentment, and bitterness are opinions that you are free to dismiss—and in so doing you take away the harm these cause. This is the attitude that modern culture calls taking things "stoically." But the true Stoic goes beyond this. You do have the right to be concerned about the injustice, but you now have a far greater chance of finding a remedy—and every right to seek remedy using your reason—if your passions are under control.

9 *Acknowledge that pain stems from our anger over an action—never the action itself.* The only pain caused by offensive behavior is our own anger. Remove the anger and we remove the pain. This advice applies also to other emotions we experience, such as grief and fear. In tempering these, we will lessen the pain and be in a far better position to deal with extreme situations.

10 *Educate the offender—the harm done is to him alone.* Although Aurelius may sound paternalistic with his ninth rule, this is not his intention. We are all children of nature. We have a duty to share the "gospel" of Stoic practice with others. The tone is gentle and compassionate. When we do correct, we do it affectionately and never with a double meaning or with a spirit of reproach.

Seventh, that it is not a person's acts which disturb us, for those acts have their foundation in our ruling principles, but it is our own opinions which disturb us. Take away these opinions then, and resolve to dismiss your judgment about an act as if it were something grievous, and your anger is gone.[8]

—XI:18G

Eighth, consider how much more pain is brought on us by the anger and aggravation caused by such acts than by the acts themselves, at which we are angry and aggravated.[9]

—XI:18H

Ninth, consider that a good disposition is invincible, if it be genuine, and not an affected smile and acting a part. For what will the most violent man do to you, if you continue to be of a kind disposition towards him, and if, as opportunity offers, you gently admonish him and calmly correct his errors at the very time when he is trying to do you harm, saying: *Not so, my child. We are constituted by nature for something else. I shall certainly not be injured, but you are injuring yourself, my child.* And show him with gentle tact and by general principles that this is so, and that even bees do not do as he does, nor any animals which are formed by nature to be gregarious. And you must do this neither with any double meaning nor in the way of reproach, but affectionately and without any rancor in your soul; and not as if you were lecturing him, nor yet that any bystander may admire, but either when he is alone, and if others are present.... [*ellipses in the original*][10]

—XI:18I

11 Aurelius injects these reminders for us to avoid flattery and competition in our dealings with others. These for Aurelius are false strategies intended to evoke emotional responses from the listener. As passions, these can only color our capacity to reason.

12 *Expect offense—it is irrational not to.* The tenth rule injects realism into the process. Ignorance and wrong actions are the way of the world—the price we pay for freedom, but according to Stoic logic, these always present us with opportunities to set the world on a right footing.

Remember these nine rules, as if you had received them as a gift from the Muses, and begin at last to be a human being while you live. But you must equally avoid flattering people and being competitive with them, for both acts are antisocial and lead to harm. And let this truth be present to you in the excitement of anger. To be moved by passion is not humane. However, mildness and gentleness, as they are more agreeable to human nature, so also are they more humane; and whoever possesses these qualities possesses strength, nerves and courage, and not the person who is subject to fits of passion and discontent. For in the same degree in which a person's mind is nearer to freedom from all passion, in the same degree also is it nearer to strength. And as the sense of pain is a characteristic of weakness, so also is anger. For whoever yields to pain or anger, both are wounded and both submit.[11]

—XI:18J

But if you will, receive also a tenth rule. To expect bad persons not to do wrong is madness, for whoever expects this wishes for an impossibility. But to allow people to behave wrongly to others, and to expect them not to do you any wrong, is irrational and tyrannical.[12]

—XI:18K

+ These meditations are helpful for anyone who uses contemplation in their struggle with addiction to drugs, alcohol, sex, or power. The approach here as elsewhere focuses on the importance of accepting what we are by nature, and reminds us always to place the needs of the mind before the pleasures of the body.

1 A life directed by self-serving pleasure is a life divorced from our first duty to humanity. Our sexual lives are clearly a part of nature. For the Stoic, sexual experience is desired by good people and bad people alike. A Stoic has no reason to reject a healthy sexual life, and most people will naturally prefer this to no sexual life at all. But for some, satisfying their sexual desire overrides everything. This compulsive behavior can play out too with food, alcohol, drugs, money, or power.

This is what the direction in the meditation is designed to question. How can I be active as a virtuous human being if I am enslaved by addiction—sexual or otherwise? Aurelius himself was married to the same woman, Faustina the Younger, for thirty years. Faustina bore thirteen children (see more on Faustina in the Introduction). There is nothing that suggests that sexual activity cannot be expressed in different ways, or exclusively in relations between a man and a woman, or restricted to procreation. What Stoic philosophy *does* maintain is that the pursuit of pleasure should not be our first priority. We may pursue pleasure—but never at the expense of our first duty to humanity.

2 This Stoic prayer focuses on a wish for release from physical or psychological pain. The prayer can also be applied to the realm of addiction. Many people with addictive behaviors continually struggle to be released *from* the addiction. This seems to be the case with many alcoholics, who fight this addiction for much of their lives. These people are often baffled by their inability to kill this compulsion and, despite their efforts, often continue their addictive patterns. On the other hand, many people with addictions learn to accept the addiction not as a weakness, but as a mysterious fact about the way they are, after which they (paradoxically) lose their compulsions by refraining from using

(continued on page 190)

☐ On Sexuality and Addiction

One prays thus: *How shall I be able to sleep with that woman or man?* Do you pray thus: *How shall I not desire this?* [1] Another prays thus: *How shall I be released from this?* Another prays: *How shall I not desire to be released?* [2]

—IX:40

drugs or alcohol, and then move on to lead exemplary lives. In these cases, even though the addiction remains, the slavery to drugs or alcohol ends. In the spirit of this prayer, they have learned not to desire to be released (from the addiction).

3 Recall that philosophy for Aurelius really means loving truth. The contemplative way approaches truth systematically. Understanding the difference between truth and falsehood is not an easy task. It requires work, discussion, reading, study, and meditation.

4 Magnanimity means high-mindedness and generosity.

5 The phrases "put off the body" and "give yourself up" entirely imply that things that happen were meant to be, they cannot be changed, and fundamentally are not in our power.

6 To "desire nothing else than to accomplish the straight course through the law" is the courage to always act with justice and fairness in everything we do. We may come under attack or persecution, but so be it: the opinions fueling these are false and we must be ready to fully accept both what we are and whatever happens to us as a consequence of personal attack or persecution.

✦ The sentiment above is reminiscent of the message contained in the Serenity Prayer used during some twelve-step addiction recovery programs: "God grant me the serenity to accept the things I cannot change, courage to change the things I can, and (the) wisdom to know the difference." The Protestant theologian Reinhold Niebuhr (see also the Introduction) wrote the prayer, but the sentiment is certainly Stoic. The Stoic understands the nature of power. It is in his nature to choose to act with courage and wisdom. The things he cannot change are beyond his power. He accepts these as his destiny and he chooses not to allow these things to restrict his capacity to act, or to disturb the serenity that flows from understanding where his choices lie.

Acquire the contemplative way of seeing how all things change into one another, and constantly attend to it, and exercise yourself about this part of philosophy.[3] For nothing is so much adapted to produce magnanimity.[4] In such a demeanor you must put off the body, and in so doing you will see that you must—no one knows how soon—go away from among others and leave everything here, give yourself up entirely to act with justice in all your actions in accordance with the universal nature.[5] But as to what anyone shall say or think about you or do against you, you should never even concern yourself with that, being yourself contented with these two things, with acting justly in what you now do, and being satisfied with what is now assigned to you; and you lay aside all distracting and busy pursuits, and desire nothing else than to accomplish the straight course through the law, and by accomplishing the straight course to follow nature.[6]

—X:11

1 This powerful meditation reminds us that when we forget what we are—and lose our capacity for contemplation—we will be troubled by wrongful acts and will feel isolated, lonely, marginalized, and abandoned. These are symptoms of anxiety and depression. For the Stoic, however, these feelings are illusions. They occur when we have forgotten these basic truths about human nature: nothing in this world can ever cause us harm. We live within a perfect community united in common purpose. Our intelligence is always invincible. There is nothing we can lose, because there is nothing that we own. Everything is in the present. The past cannot be changed. The future will be as it was meant always to be.

2 Living in accord with nature can never trouble us because nature will never cause us trouble. This may sound like circular reasoning, but it points to the Stoic belief that anything that troubles us is nothing more than an opinion that we hold. We have the power to dismiss any opinion we hold. We dismiss opinion not out of denial, but because the opinion is false. Since all anxiety stems from our attachments to false opinions, dismissing an opinion dispels the related anxiety.

For example, if I learn that I have cancer, I may be anxious for many reasons, including the fear that I may die. But death is nothing to a Stoic, other than what must happen to us all. Death is according to nature and nothing to fear. Moving from anxiety into serenity requires a shift in the opinions we hold about many things (including death) that are really only incidental to the meaning of life. In doing this, our troubles vanish.

☐ On Anxiety and Depression

When you are troubled about anything, you have forgotten this, that all things happen according to the universal nature; and forgotten this, that a person's wrongful act is nothing to you; and further you have forgotten this, that everything which happens, always happened so and will happen so, and now happens so everywhere; forgotten this too, how close is the kinship between a single soul and the whole human race, for it is a community, not of a little blood or seed, but of intelligence. And you have forgotten this too, that everyone's intelligence is a god, and is an efflux of nature; and forgotten this, that nothing is owned by you, but that his child and his body and his very soul came from nature; forgotten this, that everything is opinion; and lastly you have forgotten that every one of us lives in the present time only, and loses only this.[1]

—XII:26

Today I have got out of all trouble, or rather I have cast out all trouble, for it was not outside, but within and in my opinions.[2]

—IX:13

1 Aurelius speaks here to those who live for the praise of others. What do we gain from this if such people do not even know themselves? The opinions they offer are false; the praises they proffer come from ignorance and are motivated by flattery. Whatever the price to our personal reputation or cost to our social standing, our duty always is first to know who and what we are, and then to reach out to those who live in denial by correcting their errors.

Anyone in a position of power should be able to relate to this meditation. Flattery can be seductive. Many people use flattery to incur the favor of people who hold power over them. Employees praise their bosses, students their teachers, fans their movie and sports idols, and citizens their kings (or presidents). The wise person understands what flattery is, and knows it is false. But like an addictive drug or other pleasure, praise can be very dangerous—if we live for this praise at the expense of doing what we are meant to do in life.

☐ On Flattery and Pride

Do you wish to be praised by those who curse themselves thrice every hour? Would you wish to please those who do not please themselves? Do you please yourself if you repent of nearly everything that you do? [1]

—VIII:53

2 As human beings, each of us is a tiny part of the universal soul. This perspective is designed to discourage pride. Focusing on personal greatness seems ludicrous when we compare ourselves to the majesty of nature. The Bible records a similar sentiment when God asks the suffering Job, "Who is this that darkens counsel by words without knowledge? Gird up your loins like a man, I will question you, and you shall declare to me. Where were you when I laid the foundation of the earth? Tell me, if you have understanding" (Job 38:2–4). This confrontation leaves a cowering Job speechless.

In both of these messages human beings are confronted with crushing immensity and power. In these systems the enormity of nature (or God) would remain forever invisible to us if our lives were absorbed in self-reflection or pride. In both of these systems human worth is seemingly insignificant in contrast. But in both of these systems the divine powers show themselves as fundamentally benevolent. The tone may seem bullying in the case of Job, but the motivation is love. With pride, we miss the point of existence. We were designed to serve nature (or to praise God). The proud act as though nature were designed to serve them! For Aurelius, one thing only is great—to act as nature leads us, and nature leads us to direct our lives outwardly by discovering what nature demands and acting in all ways in accord with those demands.

3 Change is like a wide river, and we are mixed in with its waters. Holding on to false values is as futile as swimming upstream. When we "go with the flow," we will fulfill our destiny. We will also be turned the right way and be able to see where we are headed, unlike the puffed up (prideful) or fools (ignorant) who oppose nature.

How small a part of the boundless and unfathomable time is assigned to every man and woman! For it is very soon swallowed up in the eternal. And how small a part of the whole substance! And how small a part of the universal soul! And on what a small clod of the whole earth you creep! Reflecting on all this, consider nothing to be great, except to act as your nature leads you, and to endure that which the common nature brings.[2]

—XII:32

Often think of the rapidity with which things pass by and disappear, both the things that are and the things that are produced. For substance is like a river in a continual flow, and the activities of things are in constant change, and the causes work in infinite varieties; and there is hardly anything which stands still. And consider this which is near to you, this boundless abyss of the past and of the future in which all things disappear. How then are we not fools if we are puffed up with such things or plagued about them and make ourselves miserable? For they vex us only for a time, and a short time.[3]

—V:23

1 This passage employs a rhetorical repetition of the phrase "will you never" as a technique for self-examination. This meditation leads to self-knowledge and represents the first step in the Stoic journey. It is also a perfect example of Stoic prayer. Unlike a religious prayer that may begin, "God grant me," this request is directed internally, to the soul. Because the soul is connected intimately to the rest of nature, this internal dialogue is really a conversation with nature, the Stoic's concept of the Divine. In stepping through this sequence of "will-you-nevers," Aurelius offers his checklist—a set of priorities for aligning ourselves with nature's demands: Be good and simple. Be affectionate and contented whatever the circumstances. Want nothing, do not long for anything, and do not desire anything. Accept the simple pleasures. Be pleased with all that you have. Desire nothing more than what nature has assigned. Find fault with no one.

Few of us today would find any of these qualities objectionable. Such people are often described as naive. But is it naiveté if people are unaffected, simple, and lacking in artificiality? Such qualities, when combined with wisdom, are those we would expect to see in a true Stoic.

☐ On Knowing Yourself and "Wolfish" Friendships

Will you, then, my soul, never be good and simple and one and naked, more manifest than the body which surrounds you? Will you never enjoy an affectionate and contented disposition? Will you never be full and without a want of any kind, longing for nothing more, nor desiring anything, either animate or inanimate, for the enjoyment of pleasures? Nor yet desiring time wherein you shall have longer enjoyment, or place, or pleasant climate, or society of those with whom you may live in harmony? But will you be satisfied with your present condition, and pleased with all that is about you, and will you convince yourself that you have everything and that it comes from nature, that everything is well for you, and will be well whatever shall please nature, and whatever nature shall give for the conservation of the perfect living being, the good and just and beautiful, which generates and holds together all things, and contains and embraces all things which are dissolved for the production of other like things? Will you never be such that you shall so dwell in community with nature and people as neither to find fault with them at all, nor to be condemned by them?[1]

—X:1

2 The adage "The eye is the window to the soul" is by now cliché. But Aurelius brings a Stoic twist to this ancient expression and applies it to the concept of a wolfish friendship. The only true eye for the Stoic is the mind's eye, the eye of reason, and that can reveal true friends from false friends. This does not preclude the possibility that Aurelius would include the more literal possibility: that we can read human character and motivations through a careful study of voice, mannerisms, body language, and, of course, the eye. As part 9, "Society and Government in Stoicism," will explore, Aurelius places the highest importance on the cosmopolitan nature of humanity, and the social connections we maintain through our friendships and communities. Wolfish friendships will never truly harm us if we live a life of virtue (good, simple, and benevolent lives). True friends, on the other hand, are in a real sense other selves because they participate with us in that which is common to all—universal reason. Avoiding a wolfish friend does not mean banishing that relationship. We still have a duty to correct, counsel, and teach those who live contrary to nature.

Nothing is more disgraceful than a wolfish friendship (false friendship). Avoid this most of all. The good and simple and benevolent show all these things in the eyes, and there is no mistaking.[2]

—XI:15

1 This selection revisits the idea that whatever happens, happens for the best. But it suggests also that the common nature, the universal intelligence, if not benevolent, is at least not malevolent. Everything rests on our attitude. To the Stoic, good people (those who live according to nature) are immune from evil. This means that our human core—reason—is immune from the slings and arrows of fortune. Everything else we experience during the course of life, including all types of misfortune to ourselves or to others, we must regard as incidental. Nothing that happens to us or to others has any bearing on our capacity to remain fully human and completely happy.

2 Epictetus (see also the Introduction) was a Stoic philosopher. As a youth he was a slave under the tyrannical Roman Emperor Nero (37–68 CE). Epictetus was an important influence on Aurelius. This meditation captures a difficult sentiment—one every Stoic needs to hold to maintain equilibrium during the most challenging moments in life. Few experiences are as difficult as the loss of a loved one—especially a child. But Aurelius counsels that even in these times of deep sorrow, we must be ready to exercise our critical faculties. To do this we need to remember that nothing endures. Even those we are closest to might die at any time. Whatever the circumstances and however unfair these may seem, even these losses are part of nature's design, and it is essential to understand this in order to be free. We may never comprehend the details in nature's design, but we must always be prepared to give back to nature what is always only borrowed. For the Stoic, every misfortune, no matter how severe, presents us with an opportunity to act in ways that will bring peace and happiness to ourselves and to others.

☐ On Misfortune, Death, and Martyrdom

Nothing can happen to a man or woman which is not according to the nature of a human being, nor to an ox which is not according to the nature of an ox, nor to a vine which is not according to the nature of a vine, nor to a stone which is not proper to a stone. If then there happens to each thing both what is usual and natural, why should you complain? For the common nature brings nothing which may not be borne by you.[1]

—VIII:46

When a man kisses his child, said Epictetus, he should whisper to himself, *Tomorrow perchance you will die* [the man may say]. But those are words of bad omen. *No word is a word of bad omen,* said Epictetus, *which expresses any work of nature; or if it is so, it is also a word of bad omen to speak of the ears of corn being reaped.*[2]

—XI:34

3 The Stoic attitude toward the end of life is refreshing. Death is the way of the universe, according to nature, and therefore good. Aurelius approaches the question of death by looking at life as a series of small cessations in the activities of parts of a whole, ending at last with the death of the whole. Our very cells die and give way to new ones, yet our whole person continues on until the body dies. No individual cessation is an evil or contrary to nature. Therefore, the cessation of the whole cannot be evil. The phrase "nor has the one who has terminated this series at the proper time, been ill dealt with" is intriguing. It can be read as a justification for rational euthanasia, or even as a justification for the rational termination of one's own life, at the proper time. It might also be seen as offering a perspective on deaths that occur from the hands of others, either in warfare or from homicide.

+ While the Stoic would regard warfare and homicide as misfortunes, our reactions to these should never impair our capacity to respond rationally, no matter how horrific the circumstances. The attitude of the Stoic toward a killer is never motivated by revenge. This is why the Stoic views a killer with compassion. The capital punishment (execution) of a killer could never be justified as a punishment or as an instructional instrument. But it might be viewed as "according to nature" if the mind of the killer were morally and irreparably corrupt. Capital punishment in this case might be the only option left, an opportunity for the offender to perform one last noble act, by bearing his own death with dignity—a final act of virtue by the perpetrator.

The Stoic views victims in a different light. The experience of the victim would be seen as a terrible misfortune, but the death of the victim is never shameful or evil in itself. Death never opposes the general interest, nor does it harm the rational principle of the universe. Whatever happens is always in season. Death is always "seasonable and profitable to and congruent with the universal," no matter when or how it occurs.

Any one activity whatever it may be, when it has ceased at its proper time, suffers no evil because it has ceased; nor does the one who has done this act, suffer any evil for this reason that the act has ceased. In like manner then the whole which consists of all the acts, which is our life, if it ceases at its proper time, suffers no evil for this reason that it has ceased; nor has the one who has terminated this series at the proper time, been ill dealt with. But the proper time and the limit nature fixes, sometimes as in old age the peculiar nature of man, are determined by the universal nature and in a way that maintains the whole universe ever young and perfect. And everything that is useful to the universal is always good and in season. Therefore the termination of life for every person is no evil, because neither is it shameful, since it is both independent of the will and not opposed to the general interest, but it is good, since it is seasonable and profitable to and congruent with the universal.[3]

—XII:23

4   True Stoics are stateless. The first duty of Stoics is to the world—a place they see as a single and cosmopolitan (broad-based) political community. There is very little time to exercise their duty to this world. In all their actions and teachings they must "live as on a mountain" and be just in all that they do, striving to demonstrate what living in accord with nature means. No one in this political community should suffer injustice, because every human being is rightly entitled to live according to nature. All forms of discrimination—racial, sexual, economic, religious, and national—are contrary to nature. If the Stoic's example cannot be endured, she must be ready to die, "for that is better than to live as others do."

5   The invincibility of the Stoic is poignantly captured in this powerful passage. Stoicism offers freedom from compulsive behaviors, including addictions that can enslave, such as money, drugs, alcohol, fame, sex, and power. Some of these addictions were explored earlier. The tranquility that replaces compulsion brings immunity from the harsh opinion of others, whether these are expressed physically or psychologically. Concepts like these gave rise to the notion that the Stoic can be happy "even when on the rack." This attitude differs from the demeanor of the long-suffering martyr. For the Stoic, there is no sense of suffering at all. Unlike the religious martyr, the Stoic martyr—if the concept of martyrdom has any parallel meaning to the Stoic—is tranquil and serene under any circumstances, no matter how severe.

Short is the little which remains to you of life. Live as on a mountain. It makes no difference whether you live there or here, if you live everywhere in the world as in a political community. Let others see and let them understand your just example of a life lived according to nature. If others cannot endure this, let them take your life. For that is better than to live as others do.[4]

—X:15

It is in your power to live free from all compulsion with the greatest tranquility of mind, even if all the world cry out against you as much as they choose, and even if wild beasts tear into pieces the members of this body which has grown around you.... Whatever presents itself to you is never new or difficult to manage. It is always appropriate for the occasion.[5]

—VII:68

9 □ Society and Government in Stoicism

1 There seems to be a contradiction in this statement. Aurelius commands us to take pleasure and rest in one thing, while simultaneously engaging in social acts.

The apparent tension between rest and action dissolves if we recall that this place of rest is at the center of our consciousness—the mind—and the mind is at the center of reason, tranquility, and peace, yet is always active and always engaged. This is also the only place where the Stoic will find real contentment.

This tranquil space is a deeply personal place. At the same time, it is a social place, because we share our reason with the full human community. The personal and social converge in reason. But social acts are also political acts because they affect everyone. In other words, the personal is political.

2 The kingly government Aurelius mentions is not meant to endorse monarchy. Kingly here reflects on the ruling priority of intelligence or reason, within a government administered in a sage manner and following democratic ideals founded on natural law. This was just the sort of government that Aurelius tried to maintain—a representative democracy with powers shared between two houses: a Senate (with representatives from the nobility) and an Assembly (with representatives from ordinary Roman citizenry). Aurelius as emperor was commander-in-chief and carried out his duties following his Stoic ideals—in particular, his belief that living in harmony with the whole was the best thing for the good of the citizen.

✦ From other references Aurelius makes throughout the *Meditations*, it is clear that he also opposes classicism, ageism, sexism, and discrimination in general. None of these can exist in a world where ruling intelligence is shared by all. It is clear that Aurelius also opposes slavery, exploitation of labor, oppression, and censorship. Aurelius believed that everyone should be treated fairly, and he worked for the liberation of slaves and for laws that would protect the interests of minors and orphans. He was less kind to Christians. Aurelius tolerated religious

(continued on page 212)

☐ Government and Political Duty

Take pleasure in one thing and rest in it, in passing from one social act to another social act, reflecting on nature.[1]

—VI:7

From my brother Severus, [I learned] to love my kin, and to love truth, and to love justice;... from him I received the idea of a polity in which there is the same law for all, a polity administered with regard to equal rights and equal freedom of speech, and the idea of a kingly government which respects most of all the freedom of the governed.[2]

—I:14

differences but regarded Christians as immoral (living contrary to nature), though he held their activities as otherwise harmless. His attitude was likely a prejudice cultivated by his early tutor, a man named Fronton. To Aurelius, Christians seemed to seek rather than simply to endure death as part of nature's scheme. This would seem to him contrary to nature. Nonetheless, he intervened when Christians were persecuted, but only where there was evidence of recantation of their beliefs.

3 This meditation reexamines the question of social or political priority—our first duty in life. What am I doing to advance the purpose of humanity? To what extent are my personal goals interfering with this purpose? This is what he means when he asks if the social priority is "mixed with the poor flesh so as to move together with it." This is the big picture that Aurelius reminds us we must always consider; the social must always come first.

What is my ruling faculty now to me? And of what nature am I now making it? And for what purpose am I now using it? Is it void of understanding? Is it loosed and rent asunder from social life? Is it melted into and mixed with the poor flesh so as to move together with it? [3]

—X:24

4 Aurelius reminds us here that the body is a vessel. Whatever talents the body has are designed to serve humanity. We are persuaded to serve humanity by something "hidden within." These are the hidden strings that tie us to the rest of humanity. Our bodies and whatever talents we have were designed for service to humanity. Like the weaver's shuttle, the writer's pen, and the driver's whip, our talents are useless unless an animating force—the cause that moves and checks them—turns them to their designed purpose. We are free to use these gifts, and our bodies, for the exclusive gratification of our pleasures, but this is always contrary to nature. In doing this, we disconnect from the strings of nature. It is then that we are on our own. Such a life is purposeless and driven—not by reason, but by animal desire.

✦ For the Stoic, the self-serving life is so because it has never been examined. To understand what life requires of us we must first know ourselves (see part 8, "The Practice of Stoicism"). The choice to serve humanity over a life of personal gratification is never intuitively obvious. The classic model of someone who did choose service to humanity over personal gratification is the example of Socrates. In the *Apology* of Plato, an account of the trial of Socrates, Socrates tells the Athenian jury, after his guilty verdict on charges of heresy and sedition, that "the unexamined life is not worth living." For the Stoic, the example of Socrates is the example of a man who understood what his first duty was. His first duty was to the city of Athens and to conduct his life in the search of truth—a truth he understood to mean dedicating his life to the service of humanity. After Socrates was sentenced to die he had an opportunity to flee and to live in exile. He chose to remain. For Socrates, that choice would require selecting personal safety over the law, even if in his case that law, was wrongly applied.

Remember that this which pulls the strings is the thing which is hidden within: this is the power of persuasion, this is life, this, if one may so say, is humanity. In contemplating yourself never include the vessel which surrounds you and these instruments which are attached about it. For they are like to an axe, differing only in this—that they grow to the body. For indeed there is no more use in these parts without the cause that moves and checks them than in the weaver's shuttle, and the writer's pen, and the driver's whip.[4]

—X:38

1 By doing something for the general interest, Aurelius means acting in the interest of the general world community. Acting in this way means acting with virtue—justly, wisely, courageously, and prudently. In a political or social context, actions that benefit only self-interest or special interests not only oppose virtue, but they are also not within our power. Such actions will always require the collaboration of others, and clearly oppose the general interest. They never lead to happiness because they never serve the needs of the soul, where true happiness resides. They are also contrary to nature and therefore bad.

2 For Aurelius, all actions originate in reason. But the process of reason never takes place reflexively, like an instinct. It must occur with due deliberation, consideration, and purpose.

3 The theory that all matter was composed of indivisible particles called atoms was advanced long before Aurelius by Leucippus (fifth century BCE) and Democritus (born c. 460 BCE). A rival theory that all matter was infinitely divisible was advanced by Aristotle (384–322 BCE). Although Stoic physics aligned itself with Aristotle in this regard, Aurelius himself acknowledges that the question was still unresolved. There are philosophical consequences. In the ancient world, the concept of atoms led to speculation about individual atomism or even moral atomism, where each of us lives in our own moral universe. Something similar to this exists today in the modern world and began with the revival of physical atomism in the seventeenth century.

☐ Society and Social Collapse

Have I done something for the general interest? Well then I have had my reward. Let this always be present to your mind, and never stop doing such good.[1]

—XI:4

First, do nothing inconsiderately, or without a purpose. Second, make your acts refer to nothing else than to a social end.[2]

—XII:20

Whether the universe is a concourse of atoms, or nature is a system,[3] let this first be established, that I am a part of the whole which is governed by nature; next, I am in a manner intimately related to the parts which are of the same kind with myself. For remembering this, inasmuch as I am a part, I shall be discontented with none of the things which are assigned to me out of the whole; for nothing is injurious to the part, if it is for the advantage of the whole. For the whole contains nothing which is not for its advantage; and all natures indeed have this common principle, but the nature of the universe has this principle besides, that it cannot be compelled even by any external cause to generate anything harmful to itself. By remembering, then,

(continued on page 219)

4 We are all citizens in a world community. The only recipe for concord and happiness within this society is to participate fully and cooperatively in accord with the law of nature while accepting fully the responsibilities and duties assigned to us by the community. These will include paying our taxes, obeying the law, and generally placing the welfare of the community before our self-interest.

5 We are unaware of what we do when we are asleep, but some people are unaware even when awake.

6 The Greek philosopher Heraclitus (sixth century BCE) developed the concept of *Logos*. His ideas had a fundamental influence on Stoicism. Heraclitus maintained that everything comes from and is unified by *Logos*, which in turn unifies all experience.

7 Heraclitus also maintained that change is necessary and occurs only through a conflict of opposites. This is why Aurelius says that trying to oppose nature plays a role in realizing the grand design—living according to nature. This is a basis for the Stoic attitude toward dissent. Dissenting opinions serve an essential function in the Stoic search for true opinion and should never be discouraged, no matter how false they may appear. This view reappears in the nineteenth-century ideas of John Stuart Mill in his essay *On Liberty*, a work that has had a major influence on the contemporary acceptance of dissent in liberal democracies.

8 Human beings fall into two categories in Aurelius's scheme: those who cooperate and those who oppose. As mentioned in the previous note, both are required. Therefore, there is no need for you to segregate yourself from those who are not virtuous. Whatever your role in life, it will be used in the right way in realizing nature's plan.

This is provocative. Does it mean that those who fail were meant to fail? What does this say about free will? The simple answer is that free will is never suspended for anyone. No one is ever restrained from choosing virtue. The choice is a real one and is integrated into the

(continued on page 220)

that I am a part of such a whole, I shall be content with everything that happens. And inasmuch as I am in a manner intimately related to the parts which are of the same kind with myself, I shall do nothing unsocial, but I shall rather direct myself to the things which are of the same kind with myself, and I shall turn all my efforts to the common interest, and divert them from the contrary. Now, if these things are done so, life must flow on happily, just as you may observe that the life of a citizen is happy, who continues a course of action which is advantageous to his fellow-citizens, and is content with whatever the state may assign to him.[4]

—X:6

We are all working together to one end, some with knowledge and design, and others without knowing what they do; as we also do when we are asleep,[5] of whom it is Heraclitus,[6] I think, who says that we are laborers and cooperators in the things which take place in the universe. But we cooperate in different ways: and even those cooperate abundantly, who find fault with what happens and those who try to oppose it and to hinder it; for the universe had need even of such as these.[7] It remains then for you to understand among what kind of workers you place yourself; for the ruling intelligence will certainly make a right use of you, and will receive you among some part of the cooperators and of those whose labors contribute to one end.[8]

—VI:42

fabric of nature's plan. If we had no choice, we would be slaves to the ruling intelligence. As slaves, we would not be happy or capable of self-actuated virtue. That nature makes allowance for the fact that there will be those who will choose not to be virtuous in no way implies that any one of us is preprogrammed to make that choice.

9 There should be no arrogance in the way we apply reason to solving the problems of life or in doing the right thing in the interests of society. These challenges require understanding, and understanding is never easy. Knowing how to act also demands that you know yourself. This includes knowing your limitations. Aurelius is being entirely realistic about our capacities. If you are stymied about a problem, he advises you to get help, or simply to stand aside and hand the problem over to someone better qualified. But whatever the situation, you do have a responsibility to do something, and to make that decision always in the interests of society or the general good.

There are countless examples of how this advice might work in practice. People living in modern societies often encounter situations where difficulties others experience require intervention from us. Those problems may be medical, social (homelessness), legal (a friend in trouble), or personal (a neighbor in psychological crisis). A virtuous response in any of these difficulties is to take the lead, to know what needs to happen, to know where to go or whom to ask for help. You do not need to be a doctor, lawyer, social worker, or psychologist to take action. Our responsibility is to know how to recognize the need (many of us are too blindly absorbed in self-interest) and to approach whatever remedy is required with compassion and good sense. Problems arise when we ignore these situations or leave them to others. This is inaction—and for Aurelius inaction is contrary to our social responsibility.

Is my understanding sufficient for this thing or not? If it is sufficient, I use it for the work as an instrument given by the universal nature. But if it is not sufficient, then either I retire from the work and give way to whoever is able to do it better, unless there be some reason why I ought not to do so; or I do it as well as I can, taking to help me whoever with the aid of my ruling principle can do what is now fit and useful for the general good. For whatsoever either by myself or with another I can do, ought to be directed to this only, to that which is useful and well suited to society.[9]

—VII:5

10 A cylinder will roll down an inclined plane once it is released. But it must be released. In this analogy, reason (intelligence) will go through everything that opposes it once it is on a roll, or assents to action.

11 The body can do no harm to reason, but because we are free, our will is always free to withdraw its assent around anything that could be harmful to reason. For example, if injuries or diseases were bad things, then a broken leg or cancer would make us bad. Many people read injury and disease in these ways and see these as punishments. But even those injuries or diseases that we bring upon ourselves from neglect (such as lack of exercise) or habits (such as smoking) do not make us bad. The actions leading to those consequences might arise from a failure to exercise social responsibility, and these might be cause for concern, but the unfortunate consequences that may result do not make us worse. If anything, the consequences may offer us fresh opportunities for virtue.

But intelligence and reason are able to go through everything that opposes them, and in such manner as they are formed by nature and as they choose. Place before your eyes this facility with which the reason will be carried through all things, as fire upwards, as a stone downwards, as a cylinder down an inclined surface,[10] and seek for nothing further. For all other obstacles either affect the body only which is a dead thing; or, except through opinion and the yielding of the reason itself, they do not crush nor do any harm of any kind; for if they did, whoever felt it would immediately become bad.[11]

—X:33A

12 Aurelius refers to the actual physical structure of material things, including the physical human body, as its "constitution." When "accidents" occur, the constitution can become "worse." For example, we might lose an eye or an arm. But becoming worse does not mean that we have been harmed. The body is only an extension of our self. Aurelius, in fact, says that accidents can actually make us better, if we make a right use of these accidents. In other words, we can become better as human beings if we are able to transform a misfortune, such as an accident, into an advantage by becoming more virtuous.

13 The state will never suffer real harm, because the law and order of the universe—the ruling intelligence—is impervious to harm. By the same token, the citizen can never suffer harm in the face of personal misfortune.

✦ The parallels between Aurelius's world and our world—beleaguered as it is with terrorism, environmental decay, and social injustice on a global scale—are sobering. But Aurelius would see our problems, as he did his, as misfortunes arising from false opinion—misfortunes only because they make the "constitution" of things worse. Wars, terrorism, climate change, and economic crises can do terrible things to a country and to the world. These things do make things worse. But these misfortunes do not necessarily do harm to the state insofar as the state continues to respond to these crises with reason. Aurelius would also see modern problems as linked. Terrorism is rooted in social injustice. And social injustice will increase if climate change causes massive displacements of human populations.

While Aurelius would maintain that we must remain basically indifferent toward the specific harms caused by misfortunes, none of these conditions should ever be preferred. A crumbling world, a world on the edge of environmental collapse, or a world challenged by the irrationalities of terrorism and war is a world beset by misfortune.

For Aurelius, however, it is also a world of opportunities. Aurelius would maintain that seeing these misfortunes as attacks on reason would be false and might lead us to respond in inappropriate ways. Declaring a war on terror without addressing the social injustices underlying terrorism misses the mark by confusing the symptoms of terrorism with the real root causes.

Now, in the case of all things which have a certain
constitution, whatever harm may happen to any of them,
that which is so affected becomes consequently worse; but
in the like case, a human being becomes both better, if one
may say so, and more worthy of praise by making a right
use of these accidents.[12] And finally remember that nothing
harms the person who is really a citizen, which does not
harm the state; nor yet does anything harm the state, which
does not harm law (order); and of these things which are
called misfortunes not one harms law. What then does not
harm law does not harm either state or citizen.[13]

—X:33B

✦ Aurelius never really defines specifically what he means by "the state," but we can infer from what he says elsewhere that the state is a political community that must operate under the law of nature. Abusive regimes, totalitarian regimes, or regimes founded on principles inconsistent with the egalitarian and cosmopolitan nature of human beings would be seen by Aurelius as operating contrary to nature. To be consistent with Stoic philosophy generally, citizens within such regimes would be duty bound to correct or change them with whatever measures are required (see also the next chapter, "Political Activism, Criticism, and Dissent").

1 This passage discusses the question of harm at the level of the state—whether or when it does or does not occur and what response is appropriate. The passage does not address the question of war directly, but Aurelius was no shrinking violet. His wrote these *Meditations* while personally leading military campaigns that he felt were his duty. Most of those campaigns involved threats to the state by barbarian tribes (German in the north) who were pushing at the existing Roman frontiers. Aurelius was not involved in expansionary campaigns or what we would now call wars of aggression.

Although Aurelius never says what sorts of things may harm the state, we can infer from the criteria he applies elsewhere in his *Meditations* that harm can occur only if reason is somehow impaired. Aurelius consistently maintains that an individual can never experience harm because nothing can touch reason itself. But he does acknowledge that harm can sometimes occur at the level of the state. Perhaps this arises when the state is prevented from exercising its sovereignty—such was the case when Aurelius ruled. Whatever Aurelius means by state harm, his response is in keeping with Stoic philosophy. First, we must not be angry with whoever does harm to the state. Second, we must show whoever causes harm where the error is. If war became the only method available showing where error lies, then war for Aurelius would likely be seen as a form of instruction—a way of correcting error.

☐ War and Terrorism

That which does no harm to the state, does no harm to the citizen. In the case of every appearance of harm apply this rule: if this does not harm the state, neither am I harmed. But if the state is harmed, you must not be angry with whoever does harm to the state. Show whoever causes harm where the error is.[1]

—V:22

1 Aurelius pulls no punches here. He has zero tolerance for apathy, passivity, or inactivity in the political realm. Members of the human community must be socially and politically active in ways that benefit the entire human community. There is no room whatsoever in the world for the self-serving egotist. Every action taken must refer to the whole and must benefit the whole.

☐ Political Activism, Criticism, and Dissent

As you are yourself a component part of a social system, so let every act of yours be a component part of social life. Any act of yours that has no reference either immediately or remotely to a social end tears asunder your life, and does not allow it to be in solidarity, and it is of the nature of a mutiny, just as when in a popular assembly anyone acting alone stands apart from the general agreement.[1]

—IX:23

2 The criterion on which we base each decision is always found in consultation with nature; in other words, we consult our reason for guidance.

3 Blame comes from those guided by something other than reason— a peculiar leading principle.

4 When we follow the path of virtue, our nature is in common with the law of nature. In other words, the way of both is one.

Aurelius counsels us here always to do the right thing. How do we know when something is right? We know when it is according to nature. But how will we know that? Aurelius answers, when we have judged it so. Aurelius believes that every human being is capable of making sound decisions based on good judgment if reason is used in the right way. We should feel confidence in reading this. Making sound moral choices is something we can all do.

But what, then, should we do if we do not consider ourselves worthy? Aurelius answers this by telling us to dismiss this thought. Every person who consults reason is worthy. Aurelius is aware that unworthiness is common in those who may feel marginalized because of their age (very old people or very young), or rank (low-level employees in a company), or education (students in a school), or gender, or for some other discriminatory reason. Many such people will want to say or do the right thing but refrain for fear of recrimination or bullying.

What do we do if we are blamed for stirring the pot or blowing the whistle or otherwise taking some unpopular action? Justice is never served by withholding action for fear of criticism—this is always contrary to nature. We must consider the vulgar minds of those who may blame us for what we must do. Aurelius maintains, finally, that we can never be injured by anyone who acts contrary to nature. If something must be done or said, we must do it or say it. Silence or inaction never serves justice.

Judge every word and deed which are according to nature to be fit for you;[2] and be not diverted by the blame which follows from any people nor by their words, but if a thing is good to be done or said, do not consider it unworthy of you. For those persons have their peculiar[3] leading principle and follow their peculiar movement; which things do not you regard, but go straight on, following your own nature and the common nature; and the way of both is one.[4]

—V:3

Glossary □

ekpyrotic, *or "brane" model:* A modern cosmic theory pioneered by Paul Steinhardt at Princeton University and Neil Turok at the University of Cambridge. The model borrows this Greek word in its description of a theory involving an endless sequence of cosmic events, each beginning with a "bang" and ending with a "crunch." The Stoics had a similar model in which the universe underwent cyclic renewals beginning with births in fire, in a sequence repeated endlessly.

Logos: The sum total of all the *pneuma* of the universe (from which the human soul is derived) was associated with a universal or divine intelligence called *Logos* (word), the Stoic concept of the Divine.

pneuma: The fine material of nature. This material is the ingredient of *Logos*, or the active principle of nature.

Stoic commandments: The so-called commandments of Stoicism are really intellectual guidelines and are derived from reason. (1) You shall not be annoyed. (2) You shall not withdraw from others. (3) Pleasure or pain shall not overpower you. (4) You shall not be dishonest. (5) You shall not act without thinking.

Stoic contract with nature: The terms of a Stoic contract with nature can be stated succinctly. (1) Carry out all of our affairs in a spirit of justice. (2) Never put personal gain before social duty. (3) All that happens to us, for good or ill, is as it should be, and is always what is best for the world.

Stoic method: The Stoic method comprises three hierarchical stages. (1) Know and *accept* yourself with gratitude, and abandon any discontent with who you are. (2) *Examine* nature through rational inquiry and the practice of philosophy with the objective of discovering a moral basis for virtue. (3) *Act* in accordance with the laws of nature as understood from rational inquiry and live a life of virtue according to the laws of nature.

Stoic physics: Two principles were the basis of an ancient Stoic physics that divided the materials of nature into two different types. Ordinary matter was passive. Intermixed with matter was a finer or active material the Stoics called *pneuma* (or breath). Everything in nature was regarded as a mixture of these two physical principles.

Stoic pillars: Stoicism is built on a foundation comprising three distinct but interrelated disciplines: physics, logic, and ethics. Physics teaches that reason is at the center of existence. Logic teaches how to use reason. Ethics teaches how to live the good life through reason.

Stoic principles: The Stoic maintains that the following three principles are derived from reason. The first principle maintains that we are social beings. As such, we are designed for altruism because each of us is a citizen in a cosmopolitan world community. The second principle maintains that the active aspect of nature, which is distilled from the universal intelligence, or *Logos*, is rational. In human beings, the rational always takes precedence over the irrational or animal side of our nature. The third principle maintains that as rational creatures we are deeply interwoven within the fabric of a larger nature that is governed by perfect laws. As a consequence, the mind, which is derived from perfect law, is immune from harm.

Stoic psychology: Aberrations of thought in Stoic psychology present as behavioral patterns arising from compulsive noncompliance with Stoic commandments or principles. Noncompliance is generally presumed due to ignorance of nature's law or a failure of reason. The aberrations or thought patterns fall into four categories: (1) unnecessary or fanciful, (2) antisocial, (3) delusional, and (4) obsessional.

Stoic virtues: The four principle Stoic virtues are wisdom, justice, courage, and temperance.

Notes □

Introduction

1. Matthew Arnold, *Selections from the Prose Works of Matthew Arnold,* ed. William Savage Johnson. New York: Houghton Mifflin.

A Note on the Translation

1. Marcus Aurelius, *The Meditations of Marcus Aurelius,* trans. George Long, vol. 2, part 3. New York: P. F. Collier & Son, 1909–1914.

Part 8—The Practice of Stoicism: Implications for Work and Business

1. While free market economies and business have derived a great deal from the Stoic perspective on work, particularly the importance of change and hard work, this Stoic idea seems to conform to one element of the theory of work as professed by Karl Marx (1818–1883). One of Marx's more memorable slogans, "From each according to his ability, to each according to his needs!" seems to align with this Stoic view. Marx also claimed that the work done in a capitalist society separates (alienates) the worker from his nature, because the work becomes the property of others, creating an elitist class of property owners who exploit the worker's labor for their own gain. Marx, like Aurelius, believed that our labor belongs to the whole community and losing it to moneyed interests diminishes us. Aurelius would call this an evil. In response to the objection that Communism has either failed or exists only in repressive regimes, a theoretical Marxist might answer that the failed modern experiments were Marxist in name only. They also emerged historically in the wrong places, at the wrong time, and for the wrong reasons and were carried out within cultures with a long history of repression.

2. From a statement to the U.S. Senate by Charlie Wilson, Chairman and CEO, General Motors, 1955.

Suggestions for Further Reading ☐

Aristotle. *The Nicomachean Ethics.* Translated by David Ross. New York: Oxford University Press, 1998.

Aurelius, Marcus. *Meditations.* Translated by George Long. Amherst, NY: Prometheus Books, 1991.

Becker, Lawrence C. *A New Stoicism.* Princeton, NJ: Princeton University Press, 1999.

Cassius, Dio. *Roman History.* Vol. 9, books 71–80. Cambridge, MA: Loeb Classical Library, 1927.

Cicero. *On Duties.* Edited by E. M. Atkins. Cambridge, UK: Cambridge University Press, 1991.

Epictetus. *Enchiridion.* Translated by George Long. Mineola, NY: Dover Publications, 2000.

Gibbon, Edward. *The Decline and Fall of the Roman Empire.* New York: Modern Library, 2003.

Inwood, Brad, ed. *The Cambridge Companion to the Stoics.* Cambridge, UK: Cambridge University Press, 2003.

Jaspers, Karl. *Socrates, Buddha, Confucius, Jesus: The Paradigmatic Individuals.* Orlando, FL: Harcourt, 1962.

Lovelock, James. *Gaia: A New Look at Life on Earth.* New York: Oxford University Press, 2000.

Plato. *Complete Works.* Edited by John M. Cooper and D. S. Hutchison. Indianapolis, IN: Hackett Publishing Company, 1997.

Sambursky, Samuel. *Physics of the Stoics.* Princeton, NJ: Princeton University Press, 1988.

Sperling, Daniel, and James S. Cannon. *The Hydrogen Energy Transition: Cutting Carbon from Transportation.* New York: Academic Press, 2004.

Taylor, Charles. *The Malaise of Modernity.* Toronto, ON: House of Anansi Press, 1992.

———. *Sources of the Self: The Making of the Modern Identity.* Cambridge, MA: Harvard University Press, 1992.

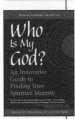

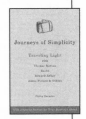

Children's Spirituality

Adam & Eve's First Sunset: God's New Day
by Sandy Eisenberg Sasso; Full-color illus. by Joani Keller Rothenberg
9 x 12, 32 pp, Full-color illus., HC, 978-1-58023-177-0 **$17.95*** *For ages 4 & up*

Because Nothing Looks Like God
by Lawrence Kushner and Karen Kushner; Full-color illus. by Dawn W. Majewski
Invites parents and children to explore the questions we all have about God.
11 x 8½, 32 pp, Full-color illus., HC, 978-1-58023-092-6 **$17.99*** *For ages 4 & up*
Also available: **Teacher's Guide** 8½ x 11, 22 pp, PB, 978-1-58023-140-4 **$6.95** *For ages 5–8*

But God Remembered: Stories of Women from Creation to the
Promised Land *by Sandy Eisenberg Sasso; Full-color illus. by Bethanne Andersen*
A fascinating collection of four different stories of women only briefly mentioned in biblical tradition and religious texts.
9 x 12, 32 pp, Full-color illus., Quality PB, 978-1-58023-372-9 **$8.99*** *For ages 8 & up*

Cain & Abel: Finding the Fruits of Peace
by Sandy Eisenberg Sasso; Full-color illus. by Joani Keller Rothenberg
A sensitive recasting of the ancient tale shows we have the power to deal with anger in positive ways. "Editor's Choice." —American Library Association's *Booklist*
9 x 12, 32 pp, Full-color illus., HC, 978-1-58023-123-7 **$16.95*** *For ages 5 & up*

Does God Hear My Prayer?
by August Gold; Full-color photos by Diane Hardy Waller
Introduces preschoolers and young readers to prayer and how it helps them express their own emotions.
10 x 8½, 32 pp, Full-color photo illus., Quality PB, 978-1-59473-102-0 **$8.99** *For ages 3–6*

The 11th Commandment: Wisdom from Our Children *by The Children of America*
"If there were an Eleventh Commandment, what would it be?" Children of many religious denominations across America answer this question—in their own drawings and words. "A rare book of spiritual celebration for all people, of all ages, for all time." —*Bookviews*
8 x 10, 48 pp, Full-color illus., HC, 978-1-879045-46-0 **$16.95*** *For all ages*

For Heaven's Sake *by Sandy Eisenberg Sasso; Full-color illus. by Kathryn Kunz Finney*
Heaven is often found where you least expect it.
9 x 12, 32 pp, Full-color illus., HC, 978-1-58023-054-4 **$16.95*** *For ages 4 & up*

God in Between *by Sandy Eisenberg Sasso; Full-color illus. by Sally Sweetland*
A magical, mythical tale that teaches that God can be found where we are.
9 x 12, 32 pp, Full-color illus., HC, 978-1-879045-86-6 **$16.95*** *For ages 4 & up*

God's Paintbrush: Special 10th Anniversary Edition
Invites children of all faiths and backgrounds to encounter God through moments in their own lives. 11 x 8½, 32 pp, Full-color illus., HC, 978-1-58023-195-4 **$17.95*** *For ages 4 & up*
Also available: **God's Paintbrush Teacher's Guide**
8½ x 11, 32 pp, PB, 978-1-879045-57-6 **$8.95**
God's Paintbrush Celebration Kit: A Spiritual Activity Kit for Teachers and
Students of All Faiths, All Backgrounds 9½ x 12, 40 Full-color Activity Sheets & Teacher Folder
w/ complete instructions, HC, 978-1-58023-050-6 **$21.95**
Additional activity sheets available:
8-Student Activity Sheet Pack (40 sheets/5 sessions), 978-1-58023-058-2 **$19.95**
Single-Student Activity Sheet Pack (5 sessions), 978-1-58023-059-9 **$3.95**
I Am God's Paintbrush (A Board Book)
by Sandy Eisenberg Sasso; Full-color illus. by Annette Compton
5 x 5, 24 pp, Full-color illus., Board Book, 978-1-59473-265-2 **$7.99** *For ages 0–4*

* A book from Jewish Lights, SkyLight Paths' sister imprint

Spiritual Poetry—The Mystic Poets

Experience these mystic poets as you never have before. Each beautiful, compact book includes a brief introduction to the poet's time and place, a summary of the major themes of the poet's mysticism and religious tradition, essential selections from the poet's most important works, and an appreciative preface by a contemporary spiritual writer.

Hafiz

The Mystic Poets
Translated and with Notes by Gertrude Bell
Preface by Ibrahim Gamard
Hafiz is known throughout the world as Persia's greatest poet, with sales of his poems in Iran today only surpassed by those of the Qur'an itself. His probing and joyful verse speaks to people from all backgrounds who long to taste and feel divine love and experience harmony with all living things.
5 x 7¼, 144 pp, HC, 978-1-59473-009-2 **$16.99**

Hopkins

The Mystic Poets
Preface by Rev. Thomas Ryan, CSP
Gerard Manley Hopkins, Christian mystical poet, is beloved for his use of fresh language and startling metaphors to describe the world around him. Although his verse is lovely, beneath the surface lies a searching soul, wrestling with and yearning for God.
5 x 7¼, 112 pp, HC, 978-1-59473-010-8 **$16.99**

Tagore

The Mystic Poets
Preface by Swami Adiswarananda
Rabindranath Tagore is often considered the Shakespeare of modern India. A great mystic, Tagore was the teacher of W. B. Yeats and Robert Frost, the close friend of Albert Einstein and Mahatma Gandhi, and the winner of the Nobel Prize for Literature. This beautiful sampling of Tagore's two most important works, *The Gardener* and *Gitanjali*, offers a glimpse into his spiritual vision that has inspired people around the world.
5 x 7¼, 144 pp, HC, 978-1-59473-008-5 **$16.99**

Whitman

The Mystic Poets
Preface by Gary David Comstock
Walt Whitman was the most innovative and influential poet of the nineteenth century. This beautiful sampling of Whitman's most important poetry from *Leaves of Grass*, and selections from his prose writings, offers a glimpse into the spiritual side of his most radical themes—love for country, love for others and love of self.
5 x 7¼, 192 pp, HC, 978-1-59473-041-2 **$16.99**

Bible Stories / Folktales

Abraham's Bind & Other Bible Tales of Trickery, Folly, Mercy and Love   by Michael J. Caduto
New retellings of episodes in the lives of familiar biblical characters explore relevant life lessons.   6 x 9, 224 pp, HC, 978-1-59473-186-0 **$19.99**

Daughters of the Desert: Stories of Remarkable Women from Christian, Jewish and Muslim Traditions   by Claire Rudolf Murphy,
Meghan Nuttall Sayres, Mary Cronk Farrell, Sarah Conover and Betsy Wharton
Breathes new life into the old tales of our female ancestors in faith. Uses traditional scriptural passages as starting points, then with vivid detail fills in historical context and place. Chapters reveal the voices of Sarah, Hagar, Huldah, Esther, Salome, Mary Magdalene, Lydia, Khadija, Fatima and many more. Historical fiction ideal for readers of all ages.
5½ x 8½, 192 pp, Quality PB, 978-1-59473-106-8 **$14.99**   Inc. reader's discussion guide
HC, 978-1-893361-72-0 **$19.95**

The Triumph of Eve & Other Subversive Bible Tales
by Matt Biers-Ariel
These engaging retellings of familiar Bible stories are witty, often hilarious and always profound. They invite you to grapple with questions and issues that are often hidden in the original texts.
5½ x 8½, 192 pp, Quality PB, 978-1-59473-176-1 **$14.99**
Also available: **The Triumph of Eve Teacher's Guide**
8½ x 11, 44 pp, PB, 978-1-59473-152-5 **$8.99**

Wisdom in the Telling
Finding Inspiration and Grace in Traditional Folktales and Myths Retold
by Lorraine Hartin-Gelardi
6 x 9, 192 pp, HC, 978-1-59473-185-3 **$19.99**

Religious Etiquette / Reference

How to Be a Perfect Stranger, 4th Edition: The Essential Religious Etiquette Handbook   Edited by Stuart M. Matlins and Arthur J. Magida
The indispensable guidebook to help the well-meaning guest when visiting other people's religious ceremonies. A straightforward guide to the rituals and celebrations of the major religions and denominations in the United States and Canada from the perspective of an interested guest of any other faith, based on information obtained from authorities of each religion. Belongs in every living room, library and office. Covers:
African American Methodist Churches • Assemblies of God • Bahá'í • Baptist • Buddhist • Christian Church (Disciples of Christ) • Christian Science (Church of Christ, Scientist) • Churches of Christ • Episcopalian and Anglican • Hindu • Islam • Jehovah's Witnesses • Jewish • Lutheran • Mennonite/Amish • Methodist • Mormon (Church of Jesus Christ of Latter-day Saints) • Native American/First Nations • Orthodox Churches • Pentecostal Church of God • Presbyterian • Quaker (Religious Society of Friends) • Reformed Church in America/Canada • Roman Catholic • Seventh-day Adventist • Sikh • Unitarian Universalist • United Church of Canada • United Church of Christ

"The things Miss Manners forgot to tell us about religion."

—*Los Angeles Times*

"Finally, for those inclined to undertake their own spiritual journeys ... tells visitors what to expect."   —*New York Times*

6 x 9, 432 pp, Quality PB, 978-1-59473-140-2 **$19.99**

The Perfect Stranger's Guide to Funerals and Grieving Practices: A Guide to Etiquette in Other People's Religious Ceremonies   Edited by Stuart M. Matlins
6 x 9, 240 pp, Quality PB, 978-1-893361-20-1 **$16.95**

The Perfect Stranger's Guide to Wedding Ceremonies: A Guide to Etiquette in Other People's Religious Ceremonies   Edited by Stuart M. Matlins
6 x 9, 208 pp, Quality PB, 978-1-893361-19-5 **$16.95**

Spiritual Biography

Spiritual Leaders Who Changed the World
The Essential Handbook to the Past Century of Religion
Edited by Ira Rifkin and the Editors at SkyLight Paths; Foreword by Dr. Robert Coles
An invaluable reference to the most important spiritual leaders of the past 100 years.
6 x 9, 304 pp, b/w photos, Quality PB, 978-1-59473-241-6 **$18.99**

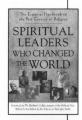

Bede Griffiths
An Introduction to His Interspiritual Thought
by Wayne Teasdale
The first study of his contemplative experience and thought, exploring the intersection of Hinduism and Christianity.
6 x 9, 288 pp, Quality PB, 978-1-893361-77-5 **$18.95**

The Soul of the Story
Meetings with Remarkable People
by Rabbi David Zeller
Inspiring and entertaining, this compelling collection of spiritual adventures assures us that no spiritual lesson truly learned is ever lost.
6 x 9, 288 pp, HC, 978-1-58023-272-2 **$21.99**
(A book from Jewish Lights, SkyLight Paths' sister imprint)

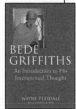

Spiritual Biography—SkyLight Lives

SkyLight Lives reintroduces the lives and works of key spiritual figures of our time—people who by their teaching or example have challenged our assumptions about spirituality and have caused us to look at it in new ways.

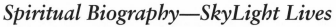

The Life of Evelyn Underhill
An Intimate Portrait of the Groundbreaking Author of *Mysticism*
by Margaret Cropper; Foreword by Dana Greene
Underhill was an early believer that contemplative prayer is not just for monks and nuns but for anyone willing to undertake it.
6 x 9, 288 pp, b/w photos, Quality PB, 978-1-893361-70-6 **$18.95**

Mahatma Gandhi
His Life and Ideas
by Charles F. Andrews; Foreword by Dr. Arun Gandhi
Examines the religious ideas and political dynamics that influenced the birth of the peaceful resistance movement.
6 x 9, 336 pp, b/w photos, Quality PB, 978-1-893361-89-8 **$18.95**

Simone Weil
A Modern Pilgrimage
by Robert Coles
A brilliant portrait of this strange and controversial figure and her mystical experiences.
6 x 9, 208 pp, Quality PB, 978-1-893361-34-8 **$16.95**

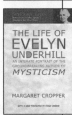

Zen Effects
The Life of Alan Watts
by Monica Furlong
Alan Watts did more to introduce Eastern philosophy and religion to Western minds than any figure before or since.
6 x 9, 264 pp, Quality PB, 978-1-893361-32-4 **$16.95**

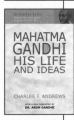

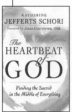

The Heartbeat of God: Finding the Sacred in the Middle of Everything
by Katharine Jefferts Schori; Foreword by Joan Chittister, OSB
Explores our connections to other people, to other nations and with the environment through the lens of faith. 6 x 9, 240 pp, HC, 978-1-59473-292-8 **$21.99**

A Dangerous Dozen: Twelve Christians Who Threatened the Status Quo but Taught Us to Live Like Jesus
by the Rev. Canon C. K. Robertson, PhD; Foreword by Archbishop Desmond Tutu
Profiles twelve visionary men and women who challenged society and showed the world a different way of living. 6 x 9, 208 pp, Quality PB, 978-1-59473-298-0 **$16.99**

Decision Making & Spiritual Discernment: The Sacred Art of Finding Your Way *by Nancy L. Bieber*
Presents three essential aspects of Spirit-led decision making: willingness, attentiveness and responsiveness. 5½ x 8½, 208 pp, Quality PB, 978-1-59473-289-8 **$16.99**

Laugh Your Way to Grace: Reclaiming the Spiritual Power of Humor
by Rev. Susan Sparks A powerful, humorous case for laughter as a spiritual, healing path. 6 x 9, 176 pp, Quality PB, 978-1-59473-280-5 **$16.99**

Living into Hope: A Call to Spiritual Action for Such a Time as This
by Rev. Dr. Joan Brown Campbell; Foreword by Karen Armstrong
A visionary minister speaks out on the pressing issues that face us today, offering inspiration and challenge. 6 x 9, 208 pp, HC, 978-1-59473-283-6 **$21.99**

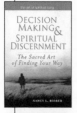

Claiming Earth as Common Ground: The Ecological Crisis through the Lens of Faith
by Andrea Cohen-Kiener; Foreword by Rev. Sally Bingham
6 x 9, 192 pp, Quality PB, 978-1-59473-261-4 **$16.99**

Bread, Body, Spirit: Finding the Sacred in Food
Edited and with Introductions by Alice Peck 6 x 9, 224 pp, Quality PB, 978-1-59473-242-3 **$19.99**

Creating a Spiritual Retirement: A Guide to the Unseen Possibilities in Our Lives
by Molly Srode 6 x 9, 208 pp, b/w photos, Quality PB, 978-1-59473-050-4 **$14.99**

Creative Aging: Rethinking Retirement and Non-Retirement in a Changing World
by Marjory Zoet Bankson 6 x 9, 160 pp, Quality PB, 978-1-59473-281-2 **$16.99**

Keeping Spiritual Balance as We Grow Older: More than 65 Creative Ways to Use Purpose, Prayer, and the Power of Spirit to Build a Meaningful Retirement
by Molly and Bernie Srode 8 x 8, 224 pp, Quality PB, 978-1-59473-042-9 **$16.99**

Hearing the Call across Traditions: Readings on Faith and Service
Edited by Adam Davis; Foreword by Eboo Patel
6 x 9, 352 pp, Quality PB, 978-1-59473-303-1 **$18.99**; HC, 978-1-59473-264-5 **$29.99**

Honoring Motherhood: Prayers, Ceremonies & Blessings
Edited and with Introductions by Lynn L. Caruso 5 x 7¼, 272 pp, HC, 978-1-59473-239-3 **$19.99**

Journeys of Simplicity: Traveling Light with Thomas Merton, Bashō, Edward Abbey, Annie Dillard & Others *by Philip Harnden*
5 x 7¼, 144 pp, Quality PB, 978-1-59473-181-5 **$12.99**; 128 pp, HC, 978-1-893361-76-8 **$16.95**

The Losses of Our Lives: The Sacred Gifts of Renewal in Everyday Loss
by Dr. Nancy Copeland-Payton 6 x 9, 192 pp, HC, 978-1-59473-271-3 **$19.99**

Renewal in the Wilderness: A Spiritual Guide to Connecting with God in the Natural World *by John Lionberger*
6 x 9, 176 pp, b/w photos, Quality PB, 978-1-59473-219-5 **$16.99**

Soul Fire: Accessing Your Creativity
by Thomas Ryan, CSP 6 x 9, 160 pp, Quality PB, 978-1-59473-243-0 **$16.99**

A Spirituality for Brokenness: Discovering Your Deepest Self in Difficult Times
by Terry Taylor 6 x 9, 176 pp, Quality PB, 978-1-59473-229-4 **$16.99**

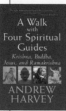

A Walk with Four Spiritual Guides: Krishna, Buddha, Jesus, and Ramakrishna
by Andrew Harvey 5½ x 8½, 192 pp, b/w photos & illus., Quality PB, 978-1-59473-138-9 **$15.99**

The Workplace and Spirituality: New Perspectives on Research and Practice
Edited by Dr. Joan Marques, Dr. Satinder Dhiman and Dr. Richard King
6 x 9, 256 pp, HC, 978-1-59473-260-7 **$29.99**

Women's Interest

Women, Spirituality and Transformative Leadership
Where Grace Meets Power
Edited by Kathe Schaaf, Kay Lindahl, Kathleen S. Hurty, PhD, and Reverend Guo Cheen
A dynamic conversation on the power of women's spiritual leadership and its emerging patterns of transformation.
6 x 9, 288 pp, Hardcover, 978-1-59473-313-0 **$24.99**

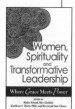

Spiritually Healthy Divorce: Navigating Disruption with Insight & Hope
by Carolyne Call A spiritual map to help you move through the twists and turns of divorce. 6 x 9, 224 pp, Quality PB, 978-1-59473-288-1 **$16.99**

New Feminist Christianity: Many Voices, Many Views
Edited by Mary E. Hunt and Diann L. Neu
Insights from ministers and theologians, activists and leaders, artists and liturgists who are shaping the future. Taken together, their voices offer a starting point for building new models of religious life and worship.
6 x 9, 384 pp, HC, 978-1-59473-285-0 **$24.99**

New Jewish Feminism: Probing the Past, Forging the Future
Edited by Rabbi Elyse Goldstein; Foreword by Anita Diamant
Looks at the growth and accomplishments of Jewish feminism and what they mean for Jewish women today and tomorrow. Features the voices of women from every area of Jewish life, addressing the important issues that concern Jewish women.
6 x 9, 480 pp, Quality PB, 978-1-58023-448-1 **$19.99**; HC, 978-1-58023-359-0 **$24.99***

Bread, Body, Spirit: Finding the Sacred in Food
Edited and with Introductions by Alice Peck 6 x 9, 224 pp, Quality PB, 978-1-59473-242-3 **$19.99**

Dance—The Sacred Art: The Joy of Movement as a Spiritual Practice
by Cynthia Winton-Henry 5½ x 8½, 224 pp, Quality PB, 978-1-59473-268-3 **$16.99**

Daughters of the Desert: Stories of Remarkable Women from Christian, Jewish and Muslim Traditions
by Claire Rudolf Murphy, Meghan Nuttall Sayres, Mary Cronk Farrell, Sarah Conover and Betsy Wharton
5½ x 8¼, 192 pp, Illus., Quality PB, 978-1-59473-106-8 **$14.99** Inc. reader's discussion guide

The Divine Feminine in Biblical Wisdom Literature
Selections Annotated & Explained
Translation & Annotation by Rabbi Rami Shapiro; Foreword by Rev. Cynthia Bourgeault, PhD
5½ x 8½, 240 pp, Quality PB, 978-1-59473-109-9 **$16.99**

Divining the Body: Reclaim the Holiness of Your Physical Self
by Jan Phillips 8 x 8, 256 pp, Quality PB, 978-1-59473-080-1 **$16.99**

Honoring Motherhood: Prayers, Ceremonies & Blessings
Edited and with Introductions by Lynn L. Caruso 5 x 7¼, 272 pp, HC, 978-1-59473-239-3 **$19.99**

Next to Godliness: Finding the Sacred in Housekeeping
Edited by Alice Peck 6 x 9, 224 pp, Quality PB, 978-1-59473-214-0 **$19.99**

ReVisions: Seeing Torah through a Feminist Lens
by Rabbi Elyse Goldstein 5½ x 8½, 224 pp, Quality PB, 978-1-58023-117-6 **$16.95***

The Triumph of Eve & Other Subversive Bible Tales
by Matt Biers-Ariel 5½ x 8½, 192 pp, Quality PB, 978-1-59473-176-1 **$14.99**

White Fire: A Portrait of Women Spiritual Leaders in America
by Malka Drucker; Photos by Gay Block 7 x 10, 320 pp, b/w photos, HC, 978-1-893361-64-5 **$24.95**

Woman Spirit Awakening in Nature: Growing Into the Fullness of Who You Are
by Nancy Barrett Chickerneo, PhD; Foreword by Eileen Fisher
8 x 8, 224 pp, b/w illus., Quality PB, 978-1-59473-250-8 **$16.99**

Women of Color Pray: Voices of Strength, Faith, Healing, Hope and Courage
Edited and with Introductions by Christal M. Jackson
5 x 7¼, 208 pp, Quality PB, 978-1-59473-077-1 **$15.99**

The Women's Torah Commentary: New Insights from Women Rabbis on the
54 Weekly Torah Portions *Edited by Rabbi Elyse Goldstein*
6 x 9, 496 pp, Quality PB, 978-1-58023-370-5 **$19.99**; HC, 978-1-58023-076-6 **$34.95***

* A book from Jewish Lights, SkyLight Paths' sister imprint

Prayer / Meditation

Sacred Attention: A Spiritual Practice for Finding God in the Moment
by Margaret D. McGee
Framed on the Christian liturgical year, this inspiring guide explores ways to develop a practice of attention as a means of talking—and listening—to God.
6 x 9, 144 pp, Quality PB, 978-1-59473-291-1 **$16.99**

Women of Color Pray: Voices of Strength, Faith, Healing, Hope and Courage
Edited and with Introductions by Christal M. Jackson
Through these prayers, poetry, lyrics, meditations and affirmations, you will share in the strong and undeniable connection women of color share with God.
5 x 7¼, 208 pp, Quality PB, 978-1-59473-077-1 **$15.99**

Secrets of Prayer: A Multifaith Guide to Creating Personal Prayer in Your Life *by Nancy Corcoran, CSJ*
This compelling, multifaith guidebook offers you companionship and encouragement on the journey to a healthy prayer life. 6 x 9, 160 pp, Quality PB, 978-1-59473-215-7 **$16.99**

Prayers to an Evolutionary God
by William Cleary; Afterword by Diarmuid O'Murchu
Inspired by the spiritual and scientific teachings of Diarmuid O'Murchu and Teilhard de Chardin, reveals that religion and science can be combined to create an expanding view of the universe—an evolutionary faith.
6 x 9, 208 pp, HC, 978-1-59473-006-1 **$21.99**

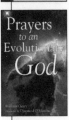

The Art of Public Prayer, 2nd Edition: Not for Clergy Only
by Lawrence A. Hoffman, PhD 6 x 9, 288 pp, Quality PB, 978-1-893361-06-5 **$19.99**

A Heart of Stillness: A Complete Guide to Learning the Art of Meditation
by David A. Cooper 5½ x 8½, 272 pp, Quality PB, 978-1-893361-03-4 **$18.99**

Meditation without Gurus: A Guide to the Heart of Practice
by Clark Strand 5½ x 8½, 192 pp, Quality PB, 978-1-893361-93-5 **$16.95**

Praying with Our Hands: 21 Practices of Embodied Prayer from the World's Spiritual Traditions *by Jon M. Sweeney; Photos by Jennifer J. Wilson; Foreword by Mother Tessa Bielecki; Afterword by Taitetsu Unno, PhD*
8 x 8, 96 pp, 22 duotone photos, Quality PB, 978-1-893361-16-4 **$16.95**

Three Gates to Meditation Practice: A Personal Journey into Sufism, Buddhism, and Judaism *by David A. Cooper* 5½ x 8½, 240 pp, Quality PB, 978-1-893361-22-5 **$16.95**

Prayer / M. Basil Pennington, OCSO

Finding Grace at the Center, 3rd Edition: The Beginning of Centering Prayer *with Thomas Keating, OCSO, and Thomas E. Clarke, SJ; Foreword by Rev. Cynthia Bourgeault, PhD* A practical guide to a simple and beautiful form of meditative prayer. 5 x 7¼, 128 pp, Quality PB, 978-1-59473-182-2 **$12.99**

The Monks of Mount Athos: A Western Monk's Extraordinary Spiritual Journey on Eastern Holy Ground *Foreword by Archimandrite Dionysios*
Explores the landscape, monastic communities and food of Athos.
6 x 9, 352 pp, Quality PB, 978-1-893361-78-2 **$18.95**

Psalms: A Spiritual Commentary *Illus. by Phillip Ratner*
Reflections on some of the most beloved passages from the Bible's most widely read book. 6 x 9, 176 pp, 24 full-page b/w illus., Quality PB, 978-1-59473-234-8 **$16.99**

The Song of Songs: A Spiritual Commentary *Illus. by Phillip Ratner*
Explore the Bible's most challenging mystical text.
6 x 9, 160 pp, 14 full-page b/w illus., Quality PB, 978-1-59473-235-5 **$16.99**
HC, 978-1-59473-004-7 **$19.99**

Spiritual Practice

Fly-Fishing—The Sacred Art: Casting a Fly as a Spiritual Practice
by Rabbi Eric Eisenkramer and Rev. Michael Attas, MD; Foreword by Chris Wood, CEO, Trout Unlimited; Preface by Lori Simon, executive director, Casting for Recovery
Shares what fly-fishing can teach you about reflection, awe and wonder; the benefits of solitude; the blessing of community and the search for the Divine.
5½ x 8½, 160 pp, Quality PB, 978-1-59473-299-7 **$16.99**

Lectio Divina—The Sacred Art: Transforming Words & Images into Heart-Centered Prayer *by Christine Valters Paintner, PhD*
Expands the practice of sacred reading beyond scriptural texts and makes it accessible in contemporary life. 5½ x 8½, 240 pp, Quality PB, 978-1-59473-300-0 **$16.99**

Haiku—The Sacred Art: A Spiritual Practice in Three Lines
by Margaret D. McGee 5½ x 8½, 192 pp, Quality PB, 978-1-59473-269-0 **$16.99**

Dance—The Sacred Art: The Joy of Movement as a Spiritual Practice
by Cynthia Winton-Henry 5½ x 8½, 224 pp, Quality PB, 978-1-59473-268-3 **$16.99**

Spiritual Adventures in the Snow: Skiing & Snowboarding as Renewal for Your Soul
by Dr. Marcia McFee and Rev. Karen Foster; Foreword by Paul Arthur
5½ x 8½, 208 pp, Quality PB, 978-1-59473-270-6 **$16.99**

Divining the Body: Reclaim the Holiness of Your Physical Self *by Jan Phillips*
8 x 8, 256 pp, Quality PB, 978-1-59473-080-1 **$16.99**

Everyday Herbs in Spiritual Life: A Guide to Many Practices
by Michael J. Caduto; Foreword by Rosemary Gladstar
7 x 9, 208 pp, 20+ b/w illus., Quality PB, 978-1-59473-174-7 **$16.99**

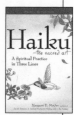

Giving—The Sacred Art: Creating a Lifestyle of Generosity
by Lauren Tyler Wright 5½ x 8½, 208 pp, Quality PB, 978-1-59473-224-9 **$16.99**

Hospitality—The Sacred Art: Discovering the Hidden Spiritual Power of Invitation and Welcome *by Rev. Nanette Sawyer; Foreword by Rev. Dirk Ficca*
5½ x 8½, 208 pp, Quality PB, 978-1-59473-228-7 **$16.99**

Labyrinths from the Outside In: Walking to Spiritual Insight—A Beginner's Guide
by Donna Schaper and Carole Ann Camp
6 x 9, 208 pp, b/w illus. and photos, Quality PB, 978-1-893361-18-8 **$16.95**

Practicing the Sacred Art of Listening: A Guide to Enrich Your Relationships and Kindle Your Spiritual Life *by Kay Lindahl* 8 x 8, 176 pp, Quality PB, 978-1-893361-85-0 **$16.95**

Recovery—The Sacred Art: The Twelve Steps as Spiritual Practice *by Rami Shapiro; Foreword by Joan Borysenko, PhD* 5½ x 8½, 240 pp, Quality PB, 978-1-59473-259-1 **$16.99**

Running—The Sacred Art: Preparing to Practice *by Dr. Warren A. Kay; Foreword by Kristin Armstrong* 5½ x 8½, 160 pp, Quality PB, 978-1-59473-227-0 **$16.99**

The Sacred Art of Chant: Preparing to Practice
by Ana Hernández 5½ x 8½, 192 pp, Quality PB, 978-1-59473-036-8 **$15.99**

The Sacred Art of Fasting: Preparing to Practice
by Thomas Ryan, CSP 5½ x 8½, 192 pp, Quality PB, 978-1-59473-078-8 **$15.99**

The Sacred Art of Forgiveness: Forgiving Ourselves and Others through God's Grace
by Marcia Ford 8 x 8, 176 pp, Quality PB, 978-1-59473-175-4 **$18.99**

The Sacred Art of Listening: Forty Reflections for Cultivating a Spiritual Practice
by Kay Lindahl; Illus. by Amy Schnapper 8 x 8, 160 pp, b/w illus., Quality PB, 978-1-893361-44-7 **$16.99**

The Sacred Art of Lovingkindness: Preparing to Practice
by Rabbi Rami Shapiro; Foreword by Marcia Ford 5½ x 8½, 176 pp, Quality PB, 978-1-59473-151-8 **$16.99**

Sacred Attention: A Spiritual Practice for Finding God in the Moment
by Margaret D. McGee 6 x 9, 144 pp, Quality PB, 978-1-59473-291-1 **$16.99**

Soul Fire: Accessing Your Creativity
by Thomas Ryan, CSP 6 x 9, 160 pp, Quality PB, 978-1-59473-243-0 **$16.99**

Thanking & Blessing—The Sacred Art: Spiritual Vitality through Gratefulness
by Jay Marshall, PhD; Foreword by Philip Gulley 5½ x 8½, 176 pp, Quality PB, 978-1-59473-231-7 **$16.99**

Sacred Texts—SkyLight Illuminations Series

Offers today's spiritual seeker an enjoyable entry into the great classic texts of the world's spiritual traditions. Each classic is presented in an accessible translation, with facing pages of guided commentary from experts, giving you the keys you need to understand the history, context and meaning of the text.

CHRISTIANITY

Celtic Christian Spirituality: Essential Writings—Annotated & Explained
Annotation by Mary C. Earle; Foreword by John Philip Newell
Explores how the writings of this lively tradition embody the gospel.
5½ x 8½, 176 pp, Quality PB, 978-1-59473-302-4 **$16.99**

The End of Days: Essential Selections from Apocalyptic Texts—
Annotated & Explained *Annotation by Robert G. Clouse, PhD*
Helps you understand the complex Christian visions of the end of the world.
5½ x 8½, 224 pp, Quality PB, 978-1-59473-170-9 **$16.99**

The Hidden Gospel of Matthew: Annotated & Explained
Translation & Annotation by Ron Miller Discover the words and events that have the strongest connection to the historical Jesus.
5½ x 8½, 272 pp, Quality PB, 978-1-59473-038-2 **$16.99**

The Infancy Gospels of Jesus: Apocryphal Tales from the Childhoods of Mary and Jesus—Annotated & Explained
Translation & Annotation by Stevan Davies; Foreword by A. Edward Siecienski, PhD
A startling presentation of the early lives of Mary, Jesus and other biblical figures that will amuse and surprise you. 5½ x 8½, 176 pp, Quality PB, 978-1-59473-258-4 **$16.99**

The Lost Sayings of Jesus: Teachings from Ancient Christian, Jewish, Gnostic and Islamic Sources—Annotated & Explained
Translation & Annotation by Andrew Phillip Smith; Foreword by Stephan A. Hoeller
This collection of more than three hundred sayings depicts Jesus as a Wisdom teacher who speaks to people of all faiths as a mystic and spiritual master.
5½ x 8½, 240 pp, Quality PB, 978-1-59473-172-3 **$16.99**

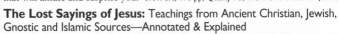

Philokalia: The Eastern Christian Spiritual Texts—Selections
Annotated & Explained *Annotation by Allyne Smith; Translation by G. E. H. Palmer, Phillip Sherrard and Bishop Kallistos Ware*
The first approachable introduction to the wisdom of the Philokalia, the classic text of Eastern Christian spirituality. 5½ x 8½, 240 pp, Quality PB, 978-1-59473-103-7 **$16.99**

The Sacred Writings of Paul: Selections Annotated & Explained
Translation & Annotation by Ron Miller Leads you into the exciting immediacy of Paul's teachings. 5½ x 8½, 224 pp, Quality PB, 978-1-59473-213-3 **$16.99**

Saint Augustine of Hippo: Selections from *Confessions* and Other Essential Writings—Annotated & Explained
Annotation by Joseph T. Kelley, PhD; Translation by the Augustinian Heritage Institute
Provides insight into the mind and heart of this foundational Christian figure.
5½ x 8½, 272 pp, Quality PB, 978-1-59473-282-9 **$16.99**

St. Ignatius Loyola—The Spiritual Writings: Selections Annotated & Explained *Annotation by Mark Mossa, SJ*
Draws from contemporary translations of original texts focusing on the practical mysticism of Ignatius of Loyola. 5½ x 8½, 224 pp (est), Quality PB, 978-1-59473-301-7 **$16.99**

Sex Texts from the Bible: Selections Annotated & Explained
Translation & Annotation by Teresa J. Hornsby; Foreword by Amy-Jill Levine
Demystifies the Bible's ideas on gender roles, marriage, sexual orientation, virginity, lust and sexual pleasure. 5½ x 8½, 208 pp, Quality PB, 978-1-59473-217-1 **$16.99**

Sacred Texts—continued

CHRISTIANITY—continued

Spiritual Writings on Mary: Annotated & Explained
Annotation by Mary Ford-Grabowsky; Foreword by Andrew Harvey
Examines the role of Mary, the mother of Jesus, as a source of inspiration in history and in life today. 5½ x 8½, 288 pp, Quality PB, 978-1-59473-001-6 **$16.99**

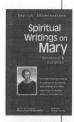

The Way of a Pilgrim: The Jesus Prayer Journey—Annotated & Explained
Translation & Annotation by Gleb Pokrovsky; Foreword by Andrew Harvey
A classic of Russian Orthodox spirituality.
5½ x 8½, 160 pp, Illus., Quality PB, 978-1-893361-31-7 **$14.95**

GNOSTICISM

Gnostic Writings on the Soul: Annotated & Explained
Translation & Annotation by Andrew Phillip Smith; Foreword by Stephan A. Hoeller
Reveals the inspiring ways your soul can remember and return to its unique, divine purpose. 5½ x 8½, 144 pp, Quality PB, 978-1-59473-220-1 **$16.99**

The Gospel of Philip: Annotated & Explained
Translation & Annotation by Andrew Phillip Smith; Foreword by Stevan Davies
Reveals otherwise unrecorded sayings of Jesus and fragments of Gnostic mythology.
5½ x 8½, 160 pp, Quality PB, 978-1-59473-111-2 **$16.99**

The Gospel of Thomas: Annotated & Explained
Translation & Annotation by Stevan Davies; Foreword by Andrew Harvey
Sheds new light on the origins of Christianity and portrays Jesus as a wisdom-loving sage.
5½ x 8½, 192 pp, Quality PB, 978-1-893361-45-4 **$16.99**

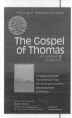

The Secret Book of John: The Gnostic Gospel—Annotated & Explained
Translation & Annotation by Stevan Davies The most significant and influential text of the ancient Gnostic religion. 5½ x 8½, 208 pp, Quality PB, 978-1-59473-082-5 **$16.99**

JUDAISM

The Divine Feminine in Biblical Wisdom Literature
Selections Annotated & Explained
Translation & Annotation by Rabbi Rami Shapiro; Foreword by Rev. Cynthia Bourgeault, PhD
Uses the Hebrew Bible and Wisdom literature to explain Sophia's way of wisdom and illustrate Her creative energy. 5½ x 8½, 240 pp, Quality PB, 978-1-59473-109-9 **$16.99**

Ecclesiastes: Annotated & Explained
Translation & Annotation by Rabbi Rami Shapiro; Foreword by Rev. Barbara Cawthorne Crafton
A timeless teaching on living well amid uncertainty and insecurity.
5½ x 8½, 160 pp, Quality PB, 978-1-59473-287-4 **$16.99**

Ethics of the Sages: Pirke Avot—Annotated & Explained
Translation & Annotation by Rabbi Rami Shapiro Clarifies the ethical teachings of the early Rabbis. 5½ x 8½, 192 pp, Quality PB, 978-1-59473-207-2 **$16.99**

Hasidic Tales: Annotated & Explained
Translation & Annotation by Rabbi Rami Shapiro; Foreword by Andrew Harvey
Introduces the legendary tales of the impassioned Hasidic rabbis, presenting them as stories rather than as parables. 5½ x 8½, 240 pp, Quality PB, 978-1-893361-86-7 **$16.95**

The Hebrew Prophets: Selections Annotated & Explained
Translation & Annotation by Rabbi Rami Shapiro; Foreword by Rabbi Zalman M. Schachter-Shalomi
5½ x 8½, 224 pp, Quality PB, 978-1-59473-037-5 **$16.99**

Tanya, the Masterpiece of Hasidic Wisdom: Selections Annotated & Explained
Translation & Annotation by Rabbi Rami Shapiro; Foreword by Rabbi Zalman M. Schachter-Shalomi Clarifies one of the most powerful and potentially transformative books of Jewish wisdom. 5½ x 8½, 240 pp, Quality PB, 978-1-59473-275-1 **$16.99**

Zohar: Annotated & Explained
Translation & Annotation by Daniel C. Matt; Foreword by Andrew Harvey The canonical text of Jewish mystical tradition.
5½ x 8½, 176 pp, Quality PB, 978-1-893361-51-5 **$15.99**

Sacred Texts—continued

MORMONISM

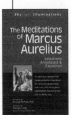

The Book of Mormon: Selections Annotated & Explained
Annotation by Jana Riess; Foreword by Phyllis Tickle Explores the sacred epic that is cherished by more than twelve million members of the LDS church as the keystone of their faith. 5½ x 8½, 272 pp, Quality PB, 978-1-59473-076-4 **$16.99**

NATIVE AMERICAN

Native American Stories of the Sacred: Annotated & Explained
Retold & Annotated by Evan T. Pritchard These teaching tales contain elegantly simple illustrations of time-honored truths. 5½ x 8¾, 272 pp, Quality PB, 978-1-59473-112-9 **$16.99**

STOICISM

The Meditations of Marcus Aurelius: Selections Annotated & Explained *Annotation by Russell McNeil, PhD; Translation by George Long, revised by Russell McNeil, PhD* Ancient Stoic wisdom that speaks vibrantly today about life, business, government and spirit. 5½ x 8½, 288 pp, Quality PB, 978-1-59473-236-2 **$16.99**

Hinduism / Vedanta

The Four Yogas: A Guide to the Spiritual Paths of Action, Devotion, Meditation and Knowledge *by Swami Adiswarananda*
6 x 9, 320 pp, Quality PB, 978-1-59473-223-2 **$19.99**; HC, 978-1-59473-143-3 **$29.99**

Meditation & Its Practices: A Definitive Guide to Techniques and Traditions of Meditation in Yoga and Vedanta *by Swami Adiswarananda* 6 x 9, 504 pp, Quality PB, 978-1-59473-105-1 **$24.99**

The Spiritual Quest and the Way of Yoga: The Goal, the Journey and the Milestones *by Swami Adiswarananda* 6 x 9, 288 pp, HC, 978-1-59473-113-6 **$29.99**

Sri Ramakrishna, the Face of Silence
by Swami Nikhilananda and Dhan Gopal Mukerji; Edited with an Introduction by Swami Adiswarananda; Foreword by Dhan Gopal Mukerji II 6 x 9, 352 pp, Quality PB, 978-1-59473-233-1 **$21.99**

Sri Sarada Devi, The Holy Mother: Her Teachings and Conversations
Translated with Notes by Swami Nikhilananda; Edited with an Introduction by Swami Adiswarananda 6 x 9, 288 pp, HC, 978-1-59473-070-2 **$29.99**

The Vedanta Way to Peace and Happiness *by Swami Adiswarananda*
6 x 9, 240 pp, Quality PB, 978-1-59473-180-8 **$18.99**; HC, 978-1-59473-034-4 **$29.99**

Vivekananda, World Teacher: His Teachings on the Spiritual Unity of Humankind
Edited and with an Introduction by Swami Adiswarananda
6 x 9, 272 pp, Quality PB, 978-1-59473-210-2 **$21.99**

Sikhism

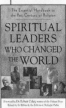

The First Sikh Spiritual Master: Timeless Wisdom from the Life and Teachings of Guru Nanak *by Harish Dhillon* 6 x 9, 192 pp, Quality PB, 978-1-59473-209-6 **$16.99**

Spiritual Biography

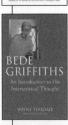

Spiritual Leaders Who Changed the World
The Essential Handbook to the Past Century of Religion
Edited by Ira Rifkin and the Editors at SkyLight Paths; Foreword by Dr. Robert Coles
An invaluable reference to the most important spiritual leaders of the past 100 years.
6 x 9, 304 pp, b/w photos, Quality PB, 978-1-59473-241-6 **$18.99**

Mahatma Gandhi: His Life and Ideas *by Charles F. Andrews; Foreword by Dr. Arun Gandhi* Examines the religious ideas and political dynamics that influenced the birth of the peaceful resistance movement. 6 x 9, 336 pp, b/w photos, Quality PB, 978-1-893361-89-8 **$18.95**

Bede Griffiths: An Introduction to His Interspiritual Thought
by Wayne Teasdale The first study of his contemplative experience and thought, exploring the intersection of Hinduism and Christianity.
6 x 9, 288 pp, Quality PB, 978-1-893361-77-5 **$18.95**